HEADWAY

UPPER-INTERMEDIATE
PRONUNCIATION

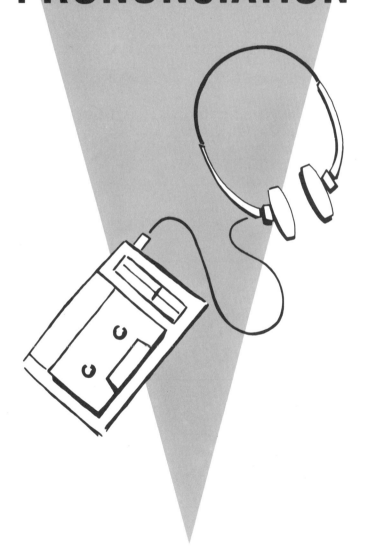

Bill Bowler   Sarah Cunningham

Oxford University Press

Oxford University Press
Walton Street, Oxford OX2 6DP

Oxford New York Toronto
Melbourne Auckland
Petaling Jaya Singapore Hong Kong Tokyo
Delhi Bombay Calcutta Madras Karachi
Nairobi Dar es Salaam Cape Town

and associated companies in
Berlin Ibadan

OXFORD and OXFORD ENGLISH are trade
marks of Oxford University Press

ISBN 0 19 433971 8

The authors would like to acknowledge the
writers of various standard pronunciation
reference books, especially Ann Baker
Introducing English Pronunciation, A. C.
Gimson *A Practical Course of English
Pronunciation*, Joanne Kenworthy
Teaching English Pronunciation, Colin
Mortimer *Elements of Pronunciation*, and
P. Roach *English Phonetics and
Phonology*. Our thanks go to Adám
Nádasdy for his learned assistance with the
Chaucer passage and in supplying texts
suitable for reading aloud. Many thanks
are due also to Sue Parminter for her
patient support throughout. We are
grateful to the people at Oxford University
Press for their tireless help and unbounded
enthusiasm. Finally, we would especially
like to express our wholehearted thanks to
John and Liz Soars for their careful reading
of the manuscript, and their invaluable
criticism, advice, and constant
encouragement.

Cartoon illustrations by:
Julie Anderson
Nigel Paige

The publishers and authors would like to
thank the following for their kind
permission to use extracts from copyright
material:

Constable publishers: from *The Education
of Hyman Kaplan* by Leo Rosten
Curtis Brown: from *The Quickest Way Out
Of Manchester* by John Wain
Houghton Mifflin Company: from
*Connections – A Short Rhetoric/Short Prose
Reader* by Daniel Brown and Bill Burnette
Random Century Group: from *The
Wedding of Zeina* by Ahdaf Soueif

Designed by Holdsworth Associates
Set by Pentacor PLC
Printed in Hong Kong

CONTENTS

* These exercises require reference to *Headway Upper-Intermediate Student's Book*, page numbers of which are given. All other exercises can be done without reference to the Student's Book.

UNIT 5

UNIT 6

UNIT 7

UNIT 8

UNIT 9

UNIT 10

UNIT 11

UNIT 12

INTRODUCTION

This book is intended for upper-intermediate level students who wish to improve their pronunciation and, at the same time, practise the new grammar and vocabulary that they have been studying. It is designed as part of the *Headway* course and each of the twelve units in this book is closely linked to the twelve corresponding units of *Headway Upper-Intermediate*. However, most of the material in *Headway Pronunciation* could easily be used by upper-intermediate students following other courses. The exercises are suitable either for classroom use or for students working independently.

● Syllabus

All the main pronunciation problems of foreign learners are covered in this book, in five sections:

1   **Sounds and Spelling**   These exercises look at sound/spelling patterns, silent letters, and individual sounds or groups of sounds that cause problems to speakers of various languages. These languages are indicated in the exercises as follows:

(D) German   (Gr) Greek   (J) Japanese
(E) Spanish   (H) Hungarian   (P) Portuguese
(F) French   (I) Italian   (Tr) Turkish

The exercises include diagrams showing how the sounds are made correctly.

2   **Connected speech**   These exercises look at the way that the pronunciation of individual words can change when they are part of a phrase, a sentence, or a longer text. In particular, they deal with weak and strong forms, word linking, and phrasing. Every other unit contains either a text for reading aloud or a dictation.

3   **Stress and intonation**   These exercises look at the most common intonation patterns and problems in English. They train students to hear different types of intonation and provide practice in some of the most common areas where problems occur; for example, showing agreement and disagreement, giving advice, criticizing tactfully, and so on.

4   **Word focus**   These exercises look at groups of words where there are problems with sounds and word stress. Usually these are Latin-based words with problematic prefixes and suffixes, but there are also homophones and homographs, compound adjectives, multi-word verbs/nouns, and lexical sets.

5   **Everyday English**   These exercises look at areas where meaning is normally internationally understood, but where pronunciation is often difficult; for example, spelling aloud, saying horoscope signs, or saying percentages.

In each unit there are exercises on each of these five areas.

● Integration with the *Headway* course

As well as providing a systematic pronunciation syllabus, the exercises in *Headway Pronunciation* aim to extend and consolidate the work done in the main *Headway* coursebook. Wherever possible they relate to the grammar and vocabulary introduced in the Student's Book, providing the opportunity for either further practice or revision. Often they make use of the Reading and Listening texts that appear in the Student's Book. The link with the main course material is indicated in the Contents Pages of this book.

● Using *Headway Pronunciation*

The exercises in this book can be used in a number of ways. All are suitable for use in class, and some include pairwork and groupwork. However, almost all of the exercises can be used equally by the student working independently – in a language laboratory, in a self-access centre, or at home. Those exercises ideally to be used in a language laboratory are indicated with the following symbol: 🎧

● Tapes

Headway Pronunciation is accompanied by three tapes, which provide all the necessary models and practice material. The tape material for each exercise is often divided into sections (**A, B, C**, etc.). The following type of symbol in the exercise indicates exactly which tape material is to be used:

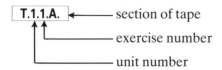

If the words that occur on the tape are not given exactly in the exercise then the tapescript is provided in the key at the back of the book.

● Key

As in the rest of the *Headway* course, the student is encouraged to work out rules for him or herself, through directed questions. The answers to these questions are provided in the key at the back of the book. The key also provides the necessary answers to exercises, as well as tapescripts not given in the exercise itself. Entries in the key are indicated with this symbol: ⚷

● The phonemic alphabet

The phonemic symbols used in this book are the ones used in all Oxford Dictionaries. More or less the same symbols are used in most other modern dictionaries and coursebooks too. Because English pronunciation/ spelling rules are very irregular, it is very important for students to know the phonemic alphabet if they want to use dictionaries independently, outside the classroom. It is also essential for students to be familiar with the symbols if they want to use this book properly. An extra unit is therefore included at the beginning of the book, designed to teach the phonemic alphabet. There are also regular transcription exercises in the Word focus exercises, to practise reading the phonemic script.

● Terminology

Many students will not be familiar with the basic terminology of phonetics. Below is a list of terms used in this book, together with examples. Use these pages as a reference while you are using the book.

Vowels There are five vowels in English – *a, e, i, o,* and *u*.

Vowel sounds There are **twelve** vowel sounds in English represented by the phonemic symbols /i:/, /ɪ/, /ʊ/, /u:/, /e/, /ə/, /ɜ:/, /ɔ:/, /ɒ/, /ʌ/, /æ/, and /ɑ:/.

Diphthongs There are eight diphthongs in English – /aɪ/, /aʊ/, /eɪ/, /eə/, /ɪə/, /əʊ/, /ʊə/, and /ɔɪ/. They are made from two vowel sounds put together.

Schwa The sound /ə/ as in *the* /ðə/. This is the most common vowel sound in English. It is **never** stressed and is often found in weak forms.

Consonants The letters of the alphabet that are not vowels – *b, c, d, f, g, h, j, k, l, m, n, p, q, r, s, t, v, w, x, y,* and *z.*

Consonant sounds The sounds made by the letters above. In the phonemic alphabet there are these additional symbols /θ/, /ð/, /ʃ/, /ʒ/, /tʃ/, /dʒ/, and /ŋ/. *c, q, x,* and *y* are **not** phonemic symbols.

Voiced sounds Sounds where the voice is needed to make the sound. All vowels and diphthongs are voiced, and so are the following consonant sounds: /b/, /v/, /ð/, /d/, /z/, /ʒ/, /dʒ/, /g/, /m/, /n/, /ŋ/, /w/, /j/, /l/, and /r/.

Voiceless sounds Sounds where the voice is **not** needed to make the sounds: /p/, /f/, /θ/, /t/, /s/, /ʃ/, /h/ /tʃ/, and /k/.

Weak and strong forms Many auxiliary verbs (like *are, was, have, can* etc.), prepositions (like *at, for, from, to* etc.), pronouns and possessives (like *you* and *your*) have two different pronunciations. In the **strong form** the vowel is fully pronounced. In the **weak form** it is shortened so that we can say the word more quickly. Often the vowel in the weak form is a *schwa* (/ə/) sound.

Example	Weak form	Strong form
have	*Have* /həv/ you been home?	Yes, I *have* /hæv/.
at	He isn't *at* /ət/ home.	What are you looking *at* /æt/?
your	Can I borrow *your* /jə/ pen?	That's not *your* /jɔ:/ pen, it's mine.

Word stress The strongest syllable in a word is the syllable with the **stress** on it. All words have a stressed syllable when you say them individually, but we do **not** mark the stress in one-syllable words. In this book word stress is marked like this:

syllable

In dictionaries it is marked like this:

'syllable

Sentence stress In the same way, some syllables in the sentence are stronger than others. In a sentence, the stressed syllables are in the words that give the main message of the sentence, usually **nouns**, **verbs**, and **adjectives**. In this book, sentence stress is marked with boxes like this:

□   □   □ □
Karen has broken her new glasses.

Main stress in sentences In any phrase or sentence there is one stress that is stronger than the others. This is the main stress. In this book it is marked with a black box like this:

□   ■
A How are **you**?

■
B Fine.

□   ■   □
A And how are your **wife** and the two
■
girls?

There can be more than one main stress in a sentence or phrase. If there is only one syllable in a phrase, then this **must** be the main stress. The main stress is often at the end of the sentence.

Intonation Intonation is the 'music' in the voice. It can go up (**rising** intonation) or down (**falling** intonation). Sometimes it does both (**fall-rise**) or (**rise-fall**). The main intonation always comes with the main stress in the sentence. In this book intonation is shown like this:

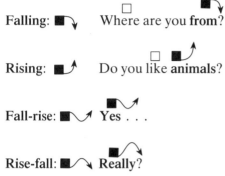

Word linking This often happens when people are speaking fast. The sounds of one word change a little so that we can say it together with the next word more quickly. There are four main types of word linking:

1 When the sound at the end of the first word moves onto the front of the next word:

      t
Get   out!

2 When the sound at the end of the first word disappears:

I've foun**d** the money.

3 When the sound at the end of the first word changes:

/ɡ/
You shoul**d** go home.

4 When there is an extra / w /, / j / or / r / sound between the two words:

Here **we**   are.
/ j /

Go   away!
/ w /

Africa   and Asia.
/ r /

THE PHONEMIC ALPHABET

Introduction

Unit Zero is intended for students who do **not** already know the phonemic symbols used in English. If you already know them but would like to revise them you should go straight to 0.6. Sounds that cause particular problems are practised elsewhere in the book, not here.

It is important to learn the phonemic alphabet because the relationship between spelling and pronunciation is so irregular in English. With the phonemic alphabet, you can work out pronunciation for yourself from the dictionary. It is also essential for using this book.

The phonemic symbols and spellings used in this book are the same as those used in the *Oxford Advanced Learner's Dictionary* (A. S. Hornby, Oxford University Press). More or less the same symbols are used in most other modern dictionaries and textbooks.

It is not difficult to learn the phonemic alphabet. However, it is probably best **not** to try to learn all of it together. You are advised to do these six exercises on separate days. When you go on to the next exercise, it is a good idea to revise the symbols that you have already learned.

1 Vowels (1)

1 **T.0.1.A.** Listen to the following pairs of sounds. Can you hear the difference between each pair?

/ i: / <u>see</u>   / ɪ / s<u>i</u>t
/ u: / t<u>oo</u>   / ʊ / p<u>u</u>t
/ ɔ: / s<u>aw</u>   / ɒ / g<u>o</u>t

2 Listen again and repeat. Try to memorize the symbol for each sound.

3 What do the following symbols transcribe?

a. / pɒt /   *pot*   i. / fi: l / _____
b. / bɪl / _____   j. / si: t / _____
c. / dɔ: / _____   k. / sɪk / _____
d. / ti: / _____   l. / bɔ: t / _____
e. / skɒt / _____   m. / wʊl / _____
f. / pʊl / _____   n. / tru: / _____
g. / fu: d / _____   o. / sɔ: t / _____
h. / hu: / _____   p. / kʊd / _____

⚷—0

4 **T.0.1.B.** Listen and write in the correct symbol for the word you hear.

a. God / g___ d /   g. bit / b___ t /
b. foot / f___ t /   h. boot / b___ t /
c. feet / f___ t /   i. book / b___ k /
d. do / d___ /   j. worn / w___ n /
e. lead / l___ d /   k. fit / f___ t /
f. four / f___ /   l. what / w___ t /

⚷—0

2 Vowels (2)

1 **T.0.2.A.** Listen to the following pairs of sounds. Can you hear the difference between the vowel sounds in each pair?

/ e / te̲n   / æ / ha̲t
/ ɑ: / a̲rm   / ʌ / cu̲p
/ ɜ: / fu̲r   / ə / a̲go

2 Listen again and repeat. Try to memorize the symbol for each sound.

What are the following professions?

a. / nɜ: s /   _____

b. / 'bʌtlə /   _____

c. / 'æktə /   _____

d. / 'æktrəs /   _____

e. / 'fɑ: mə /   _____

f. / 'wɜ: kə /   _____

g. / 'dɑ:nsə /   _____

h. / 'plʌmə /   _____

i. / 'sekrətrɪ /   _____

j. / 'bɑ: mən /   _____

π—0

3 **T.0.2.B.** Listen and match the words in each group to the correct transcription on the right.

1. bell   a. / bɪl /
   bull   b. / bʊl /
   bill   c. / bel /
   ball   d. / bɔ: l /

2. tool   a. / fɔ: l /
   full   b. / fel /
   fell   c. / fu: l /
   fall   d. / fʊl /

3. hat   a. / hɑ: t /
   hut   b. / hɜ: t /
   hurt   c. / hæt /
   heart   d. / hʌt /

4. purse   a. / pɜ: s /
   puss   b. / pɑ: s /
   pass   c. / pi: s /
   piece   d. / pʊs /

5. fist   a. / fi:st /
   fast   b. / fɑ: st /
   first   c. / fɪst /
   feast   d. / fɜ: st /

6. cot   a. / kɔ: t /
   court   b. / kæt /
   cat   c. / kɒt /
   cut   d. / kʌt /

π—0

3 Consonants

1 **T.0.3.A.** Many of the symbols for the consonants are easy to recognize. This is how they sound in English:

/ p / pe̲n   / s / s̲o
/ b / ba̲d   / z / z̲oo
/ t / te̲a   / h / h̲ow
/ d / di̲d   / m / m̲an
/ k / ca̲t   / n / n̲o
/ g / go̲t   / l / l̲eg
/ f / fa̲ll   / r / r̲ed
/ v / v̲oice   / w / w̲et

2 Listen again and mark with a * any of the consonants that sound **very** different in your language. (Most of them will sound a **little** different.) Try to memorize the consonants that you have marked.

3 **T.0.3.B.** The following consonants are more difficult:

/ θ / th̲in   / ð / th̲en
/ ʃ / sh̲e   / ʒ / vi̲sion
/ tʃ / ch̲in   / dʒ / J̲une
/ ŋ / si̲ng   / j / y̲es

Listen again and try to memorize them.

4 Cover the words and symbols in 3 above and try to match the symbols to the words.

/ ŋ /   yes
/ ʃ /   vision
/ dʒ /   then
/ θ /   chin
/ tʃ /   thin
/ j /   sing
/ ð /   she
/ ʒ /   June

Check your answers.

5 T.0.3.C. Listen to the words and circle the correct transcription.

1. washing

a. / 'wætʃɪŋ / c. / 'wɒtʃɪŋ /
b. / 'wɒʃɪŋ / d. / 'wæʃɪŋ /

2. chip

a. / tʃɪp / c. / ʃɪp /
b. / tʃi: p / d. / ʃi: p /

3. these

a. / θi: z / c. / θɪz /
b. / ðɪz / d. / ði: z /

4. thought

a. / θɒt / c. / θɔ: t /
b. / ðɔ: t / d. / ðɒt /

5. thank

a. / θænk / c. / ðæŋk /
b. / ðænk / d. / θæŋk /

6. short

a. / tʃɔ: t / c. / ʃɒt /
b. / ʃɔ: t / d. / ʃɜ: t /

7. use

a. / ju: z / c. / u: z /
b. / dʒu: z / d. / u: s /

8. jaw

a. / tʃɔ: / c. / jɔ: /
b. / dʒɔ: / d. / dʒɔ: w /

4 Diphthongs (1)

1 T.0.4. Diphthongs consist of two vowel sounds put together. Listen to the way the following diphthongs are made.

/ eɪ / page / aʊ / now / aɪ / five / ɔɪ / join

2 Listen again and repeat. Try to memorize the symbol for each diphthong.

3 Transcribe the following words.

a. / bɔɪ / ______ j. / tʃaɪld / ______
b. / weɪv / ______ k. / 'weɪdʒɪz / ______
c. / haɪd / ______ l. / ʃaʊt / ______
d. / deɪ / ______ m. / tʃɔɪs / ______
e. / haʊ / ______ n. / ʃaɪ / ______
f. / raɪt / ______ o. / 'deɪndʒə / ______
g. / faʊnd / ______ p. / en'dʒɔɪd / ______
h. / 'bɔɪlɪŋ / ______ q. / 'aɪðə / ______
i. / ðeɪ / ______ r. / 'ʃaʊə / ______

4 Work with a partner. Can you think of other words with these diphthong sounds that are spelled in the same way?

Examples
boy–toy
found–sound

Check your answers in a dictionary.

5 Diphthongs (2)

1 **T.0.5.A.** Listen to how these diphthongs are made.

/əʊ/ h<u>o</u>me   /ɪə/ n<u>ear</u>

/eə/ h<u>air</u>   /ʊə/ p<u>ure</u>*

* This diphthong is very rare. Some native speakers of English never use it. They use /ɔ:/ instead.

2 Listen again and repeat. Try to memorize the symbol for each diphthong.

3 **T.0.5.B.** Listen to the words on the left and circle the correct transcription on the right.

1.	pair	a.	/peɪ/	b.	(/peə/)
2.	rice	a.	/reɪs/	b.	/raɪs/
3.	grow	a.	/grəʊ/	b.	/greɪ/
4.	care	a.	/keə/	b.	/kaʊ/
5.	boil	a.	/bəʊl/	b.	/bɔɪl/
6.	loud	a.	/ləʊd/	b.	/laʊd/
7.	day	a.	/daɪ/	b.	/deɪ/
8.	beer	a.	/bɪə/	b.	/beə/
9.	toe	a.	/tʊə/	b.	/təʊ/
10.	night	a.	/naɪt/	b.	/nəʊt/
11.	dear	a.	/deə/	b.	/dɪə/
12.	fare	a.	/feə/	b.	/fɪə/

π—0

4 What is the other word in each pair?

π—0

5 Cover the words and symbols in 1 above. Try to match the symbol on the left with the word containing it on the right.

/eɪ/	pure
/əʊ/	five
/aɪ/	now
/aʊ/	home
/ɔɪ/	hair
/ɪə/	join
/eə/	near
/ʊə/	page

Check your answers.

6 Revision

1 Work in pairs. Look at the list of phonemic symbols on page 84 and write down ten symbols that you think your partner might still confuse. Show your partner the symbols and ask him or her to give you a word with that sound in it. If you disagree about any words then check them in the dictionary.

2 **T.0.6.** All the words below are parts of the body. Can you remember what they all mean?

Listen and fill in the missing symbols in the transcriptions.

a. face /f___s/

b. eyes /___z/

c. ears /___z/

d. nose /n___z/

e. cheeks /tʃ___ks/

f. mouth /m___θ/

g. teeth /ti:___/

h. tongue /tʌ___/

i. chin /___ɪn/

j. jaw /___ɔ:/

k. shoulder /'___əʊld___/

l. arm /___m/

m. elbow /'elb___/

n. hand /h___nd/

o. thumb /θ___m/

p. finger /'fɪ___g___/

q. chest /___est/

r. waist /w___st/

s. hips /h___ps/

t. bottom /'b___t___m/

u. thigh /___aɪ/

v. knee /n___/

w. shin /___ɪn/

x. ankle /___ŋkl/

y. foot /f___t/

π—0

UNIT 1

● Sounds and spelling

1 The sounds / i: /, / ɪ /, and / aɪ /
Ⓔ Ⓕ Ⓖⓡ Ⓗ Ⓘ Ⓙ Ⓟ Ⓣⓡ

1 | **T.1.1.A.** | Here are some lines from Geoffrey Chaucer's famous poem *The Canterbury Tales*, written in 1380. Chaucer's English looks quite similar to modern English, but the pronunciation was very different. Listen to an actor talking about the passage and circle the words he mentions.

A knight ther was and that a worthy man
That, fro the time that he first bigan
to riden out, he loved chivalrye,
Trouthe and honour, fredom and curteisye.
⊓─0

In Chaucer's day words were written as they were pronounced. Today's English is not so phonetic. This is because, over the centuries, the pronunciation of certain words has changed while their spelling has remained fixed.

2 | **T.1.1.B.** | The following words come from the Reading text on page 2 of the Student's Book. Listen to the first three examples and make sure you can hear the difference between the three vowel sounds. Then listen to the others and mark them / ɪ /, / aɪ / or / i: /.

/ i: /
a. fr<u>ee</u>   g. b<u>i</u>lingual

/ ɪ /
b. b<u>e</u>gan   h. r<u>e</u>cent

/ aɪ /
c. t<u>i</u>me   i. w<u>i</u>despread

d. sp<u>ea</u>k   j. b<u>u</u>siness

e. dr<u>ie</u>d   k. lang<u>ua</u>ge

f. p<u>eo</u>ple   l. p<u>i</u>d<u>gi</u>n
⊓─0

3 Practise making the sounds. To make the sound / i: / your tongue should be high at the front of your mouth and your lips should be spread as if you are smiling, like this:

/ i: /

/ i: / is a **long** sound.

1

To make the sound / ɪ / your tongue should be a little lower and your lips a little rounder like this:

/ ɪ / is a **short** sound.

To make the sound / aɪ / first make the sound / ɑː /. Your tongue should be low in your mouth and your lips should be open. Then add a short / ɪ / sound, like this:

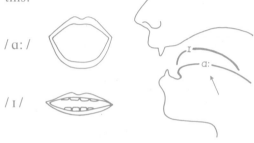

/ aɪ / is a **long** sound – it is a *diphthong*.

Listen and repeat the words paying attention to your pronunciation of the vowel sounds.

4   Now look at these words and phrases and try to say which of the three vowel sounds they contain.

> English teachers   Italian ice cream
> Greek islands   Indian tea
> Swiss cheese   Swedish films
> Irish whiskey   Egyptian spices

T.1.1.C.   Listen again and practise the phrases saying the vowels correctly.

---

2 The silent '-*e*' rule

1   **T.1.2.A.**   Listen to these pairs of words. What happens in each case when *e* is added?

A
win . . . ⎱
bit . . . ⎰ /ɪ/

B
wine ⎱
bite ⎰ ___

mad . . . ⎱
Dan . . . ⎰ ___

made ⎱
Dane ⎰ ___

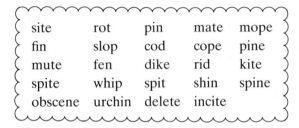

hop . . . ⎱ ___
not . . . ⎰

hope ⎱ ___
note ⎰

pet . . . ___

cut . . . ___

Pete ___

cute ___

Put the correct phonemic symbol next to the words in both column **A** and column **B**:

/ ɪ / / e / / ɒ / / ʌ / / æ / / juː / / aɪ / / eɪ / / iː / / əʊ /

2   Below are some more words which you may or may not know. Try to guess how they are pronounced.

site	rot	pin	mate	mope
fin	slop	cod	cope	pine
mute	fen	dike	rid	kite
spite	whip	spit	shin	spine
obscene	urchin	delete	incite	

T.1.2.B.   Listen and check your answers.

3   Notice what happens to words with a short vowel sound when a suffix is added:

-ing: get   → ge*tt*ing
            sit   → si*tt*ing

-ed: fit   → fi*tt*ed
            hop   → ho*pp*ed

-er/-est: big   → bi*gg*er   → bi*gg*est
            hot   → ho*tt*er   → ho*tt*est

Notice what happens to words with a long vowel sound when a suffix is added:

-ing: hate   → ha*t*ing
            shine → shi*n*ing

-ed: tape   → ta*p*ed
            hope   → ho*p*ed

-er/-est: late   → la*t*er   → la*t*est
            fine   → fi*n*er   → fi*n*est

4   How would you spell these words with the following suffixes?

-ing	*-ed*	*-er*	*-est*
spit	mope	fit	close
win	whip	cute	thin
cope	note	fat	mad
shop	pop	pale	sad

● Word focus

3 Grammatical and phonetic terminology

When learning a foreign language it is very useful to know some of the most important grammatical and phonetic terms for describing it. Can you transcribe the terms below? Do you know what they all mean? If not, check the meaning in a dictionary.

1. / naʊn /   *noun*
2. / vɜː b /   _____
3. / 'vaʊəl /   _____
4. / tens /   _____
5. / 'regjʊlə /   _____
6. / ɪ'regjʊlə /   _____
7. / 'sɪŋgjʊlə /   _____
8. / 'plʊərəl /   _____
9. / pʌŋktʃʊ'eɪʃn /   _____
10. / prepə'zɪʃn /   _____
11. / prənʌnsɪ'eɪʃn /   _____
12. / 'kɒnsənənt /   _____
13. / ɔː g'zɪlɪərɪ /   _____
14. / 'ædʒɪktɪv /   _____
15. / ɪntə'neɪʃn /   _____

Practise reading the phonemic script of the words.

4 Word families, stress, and the sound / ə /

1   The strongest syllable in a word is called the **stressed** syllable. All words have a stressed syllable. In word families this can sometimes change.

●● ●   ● ● ●● ●
a photograph   photographic
/ 'fəʊtəgrɑː f /   / fəʊtə'græfɪk /

● ● ● ●   ●● ● ●
photographer   to photograph
/ fə'tɒgrəfə /   / 'fəʊtəgrɑː f /

T.1.4.A.   Listen to the stress in each word.

2   Look at the phonemic spelling of the words in 1. Which sound is common in the **unstressed** syllables?

This unstressed sound is / ə /. It is the most common vowel sound in English. Listen to the words again.

3   Practise making the sound / ə /. You should make the sound in the middle of your mouth and your lips should be spread like this:

/ ə /

Listen again and repeat the words paying attention to the stress and the sound / ə /.

4   Here are some more word families. Mark the main stress and indicate the examples of the sound / ə /.

Noun	Adjective	Person	Verb
● ● ●	● ● ● ●	● ● ● ● ●	● ● ● ● ●
/ ə /	/ ə /	/ ə /	/ ə /
industry	industrial	industrialist	industrialize
invention	inventive	inventor	invent
competition	competitive	competitor	compete
criticism	critical	critic	criticize
politics	political	politician	politicize
nation	nationalistic	nationalist	nationalize
analysis	analytical	analyst	analyse

T.1.4.B.   Listen and check to see if you guessed correctly.

Listen again and practise saying the words that you guessed incorrectly.

● Connected speech

5 Weak forms of auxiliary verbs

1 **T.1.5.** You will hear twelve sentences. Listen to them once and say what tense the verb form is in, and whether it is active or passive.

a. _Present Simple (active)_

b. _____

c. _____

d. _____

e. _____

f. _____

g. _____

h. _____

i. _____

j. _____

k. _____

l. _____

⊓—0

2 Listen to the sentences again and write the missing words into the gaps.

a. _____ here a lot?

b. They _____ us.

c. They _____ another argument.

d. The car _____ at the moment.

e. This letter _____ two months ago.

f. That _____ me all day.

g. We _____ to help.

h. We _____ anything yet.

i. I'm sure we _____ just then.

j. I _____ home by eight o'clock.

k. They _____ a lot of problems lately.

l. We _____ for you at the entrance.

⊓—0

3 Which part of the verb forms are stressed?
⊓—0

How are the following auxiliary verbs pronounced in fast speech?
Listen again if you cannot remember.

do you / dʒʊ / or / dʒə /	I'm / aɪm / or / æm /
weren't / wɜ: nt /	were / wə /
they're / ðeə / or / ðe /	I'll / aɪl / or / æl /
being / bɪɪŋ /	have / həv / or / əv /
was / wəz /	they've / ðeɪv / or / ðev /
been / bɪn /	we'll / wi: l / or / wɪl /
we're / wɪə / or / wɪ /	be / bɪ /
haven't / hævnt /	

4 Practise saying the verbs above on their own. Then practise saying them in the following sentences. Pay attention to the pronunciation of the weak forms.

a. Do you really like Beethoven?
b. You weren't in when I called.
c. They're leaving this Wednesday.
d. She's just being difficult.
e. I was worried about you.
f. I've been waiting for you to phone.
g. We're dealing with the problem.
h. I haven't said a word to anyone.
i. I'm afraid we were too late.
j. I'll have finished typing it by lunchtime.
k. They've never been happy together.

6 Reading aloud

1 **T.1.6.A.** Listen to the following reading passage. Read the text silently as you listen.

'Vocabulary!' Mr Parkhill thought. 'Above all I must help them increase their vocabularies.'

He was probably right. What the students in the beginners' grade most needed, what they could put to instant use, was a copious supply of words: English words, words for naming ordinary objects, asking simple questions, describing everyday experiences. If one weighted the respective merits of vocabulary and, say, spelling, as Mr Parkhill had spent many an hour doing, one would be forced to decide in favour of devoting more time to the former than the latter. However basic spelling is (and to Mr Parkhill nothing was more basic) it is nonetheless not so pressing *outside* a classroom to adults who do little actual writing in their daily work and life.

'After all,' Mr Parkhill had put it to Miss Higby, 'one does not need to know how to *spell* English in order to use it!'

'Our students certainly prove that,' Miss Higby had replied.

2 **T.1.6.B.** You will now hear the same passage broken up into short phrases. Listen and repeat each phrase, paying attention to word linking and to intonation.

3 **T.1.6.C.** You will now hear the same passage broken up into longer sentences. Listen and repeat each sentence, paying attention to intonation and phrasing.

4 Now read the whole passage through aloud, paying attention to phrasing and to pace.

● Stress and intonation

7 Greetings

1 **T.1.7.A.** Listen to these three dialogues. Imagine a situation for each one. How do the people feel towards each other?

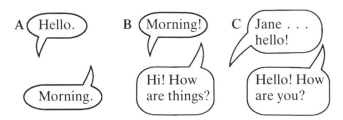

What do you notice about the intonation in each case?

2 **T.1.7.B.** Listen to the following people greeting each other and mark the dialogues * if they sound neutral/relatively uninterested (like speaker **A** above) ** if they sound friendly and interested (like speaker **B** above) and *** if they sound excited/very pleased to see each other (like speaker **C** above).

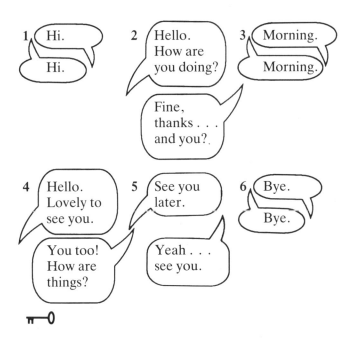

5

3 | **T.1.7.C.** | To sound friendly and interested when you greet someone, your intonation should start high like this:

Hi! . . . . . .Hello! . . . . . .Morning! . . . . . .Bye!

How are you? . . . . How are things? . . . .

How are you doing? Fine, thanks! . . . .

Listen and practise.

---

8 Main stress and intonation in questions

1 | **T.1.8.A.** | In the following questions the stress has already been marked. Listen to them, paying particular attention to the stress.

☐ = stress ■ = main stress

a. Where were you born?

b. Which countries have you been to?

c. What's your job?

d. Why are you learning English?

What kind of words are stressed?
π—0

2 | **T.1.8.B.** | Look at the following questions and try to guess which syllables are stressed. Mark the stresses like this ☐.

a. Have you got any children?

b. Are you married?

c. Do you speak any other languages?

d. Do you do any sports?

In each question there is one **main** stress. Listen again and mark the main stress like this ■.
π—0

3 | The main intonation movements in a phrase or sentence are always on the main stress. Listen to the questions in 1 and 2 again and decide if the intonation goes **up** or **down** in each group.

What kind of questions have rising intonation? What kind of questions have falling intonation?
π—0

4 | **T.1.8.C.** | Practise the questions with falling intonation. It may help just to hum the tune first – listen and try. Remember that it is important to **start high**.

☐
DE   de de   DE?

☐
Where were you born?

☐   ☐
DE   DE-de de de DE de?

☐   ☐
Which countries have you been to?

☐
DE   de   DE?

☐
What's your job?

☐   ☐
DE   de de DE-de   DE-de

☐   ☐
Why are you learning English?

5 | **T.1.8.D.** | Sometimes – when we want to show our surprise, or ask someone to repeat something – we use *Wh-* questions with rising intonation, and with a different stress pattern. Listen and mark the main stresses in these questions like this ■.

a. Where were you born?

b. Which countries have you been to?

c. What's your job?

d. Why are you learning English?

e. How old are you?

f. When did you get married?
π—0

Listen again and repeat the questions, paying attention to intonation and stress.

6 | Work in threes.
Student A – ask some *Wh-* questions.
Student B – give some surprising answers.
Student C – show your surprise.

Example A Where were you born?
　　　　　　B On the Orient Express.
　　　　　　C Where were you born?
　　　　　　B On the Orient Express.

Everyday English

9 Loan words from other languages

1 There are many words in English which are borrowed from other languages. Here are some common ones. Put them into one of the categories below.

ballet	barbecue	cuisine	gourmet
bungalow	chalet	hors d'œuvres	restaurant
casino	concerto	karate	villa

A Buildings	B Food

C Other

T.1.9. Listen and check your answers.

2 How many of these words are used in your language? Are they pronounced differently in your language or not?

Listen again and practise saying them the English way.

Can you think of any more loan words that you know are used in English? Make a list. Use a dictionary to check how they are pronounced in English.

10 Stress in numbers – thirty and thirteen

1 It is often difficult to hear the difference between these numbers. Notice the different stress:

●●   ● ●
thirty   thirteen

T.1.10.A. Listen to these pairs of numbers and repeat them with the correct stress.

30	13	60	16	80	18
40	14	70	17	90	19
50	15

What happens if you just list the -teen words?

2 T.1.10.B. Listen and circle the dates you hear.

   a. He died in 1117 / 1170.
   b. He became king in 1216 / 1260.
   c. It was published in 1719 / 1790.
   d. It was opened in 1813 / 1830.
   e. He was defeated in 1815 / 1850.
   f. It was written in 1516 / 1560.
   g. It was founded in 1415 / 1450.
   h. War broke out in 1618 / 1680.
   i. It was signed in 1713 / 1730.
   j. They were married in 1514 / 1540.
   k. She was born in 1913 / 1930.
   l. He resigned in 1918 / 1980.

Listen again and practise saying the sentences.

3 The stress on *thirty*, *forty*, etc. does not usually vary.

   ●●   ●●
He's thirty.   That's thirty pounds.

The stress on *thirteen*, *fourteen*, etc. varies according to context.

   ● ●   ●●
She's thirteen.   That's thirteen pounds.

T.1.10.C. Listen to the following sentences and mark the main stress on the -teen words.

   a. There were thirteen guests at the dinner table.
   b. He's just turned nineteen.
   c. The box contained sixteen toy soldiers.
   d. Two sevens are fourteen.
   e. Seventeen's my lucky number.
   f. I used to smoke at least fifteen cigarettes a day.
   g. She lives at number eighteen.
   h. It weighs exactly fourteen kilos.

4 Can you work out the stress rule on -teen words?

UNIT 2

● Sounds and spelling

1 The sound / h /
Ⓔ Ⓕ Ⓖⓡ Ⓘ Ⓟ

1 **T.2.1.A.** Listen and circle the words you hear.

a. hair   air   d. hearing   earring
b. heat   eat   e. heels   eels
c. harmed   armed
🔑

2 To make the sound / h / you should push a lot of air out of your mouth without moving your tongue. The sound is similar to the noise you make if you are out of breath.

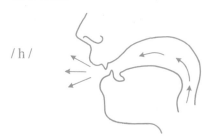
/ h /

3 **T.2.1.B.** Listen to these pairs of words, and repeat them.

hair	air	heels	eels
heat	eat	heart	art
harmed	armed	hill	ill
hearing	earring	hall	all

Work in pairs.

Student A Say one of the words above.
Student B Point to the word you hear.

4 When a word begins with a vowel sound it links with the word before:

What nice clean air!   Do you like art?

When the word before also ends in a vowel sound then either a / w / or a / j / sound is added in fast speech.

/ w /
Will you eat that soup up?
/ j /
Those terrorists can't be armed.

Mark the linking / w / and / j / sounds in the following sentences.

/ w /
a. He's got absolutely no idea how I organize things.

b. It's Harriet's free evening, and she's gone to

the opera.

c. We aren't going to hurry off to the zoo now after all.

d. Henry and I agree that you are to inherit

the antique hatstand.

e. They admire Hugh a lot. He's a handsome

boy and so intelligent too.

T.2.1.C. Listen and repeat the sentences, paying attention to the word linking.
🔑

5 Complete the rules:

_____ is the linking sound between two words when the second word begins with a vowel and the first word ends with a rounded vowel. (/ u: /, / ʊ /, / əʊ /, / aʊ /)

_____ is the linking sound between two words when the second word begins with a vowel and the first word ends with a non-rounded vowel. (/ i: /, / ɪ /, / eɪ /, / aɪ /, / ɔɪ /)
🔑

8

2 Silent letter 'h'

1 Circle the odd word in each group, and say why it is different.

heir	perhaps	whale
honest	rheumatism	when
hotel	rhyme	whisky
hour	rhythm	whole
honour	rhinoceros	white

π—0

T.2.2.A. Listen to the words and practise saying them.

2 Look at the words in the boxes above. Complete the rules:

a. *h* is usually pronounced at the beginning of a word, but it is silent in the words

_____, _____, and

_____.

b. *rh* at the beginning of a word is always

pronounced _____.

c. *wh* at the beginning of a word is usually

pronounced _____. (In some varieties of English –

Scottish, for example – it may be pronounced

/ hw /.) In words beginning with *who-*, *wh* is

usually pronounced _____.

π—0

3 Some of these words contain silent *h* too. Cross out the silent *h*s.

yoghurt	exhibition	exhaust
harmony	heiress	pharoah
vehicle	hierarchy	philharmonic
cowhide	hospital	herb

π—0

T.2.2.B. Listen and practise saying the words.

3 The sounds / æ / and / ʌ /

(E) (F) (Gr) (I) (J) (Tr)

1 **T.2.3.A.** Listen and circle the words you hear.

a. cap — cup
b. bag — bug
c. cat — cut
d. rag — rug
e. ankle — uncle

π—0

2 Practise making the sounds.

To make the sound / æ /, your mouth should be open like this, and your tongue should be down at the front of your mouth:

/ æ /

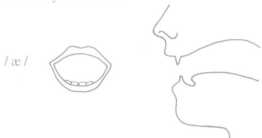

To make the sound / ʌ / your mouth should be less open, and your tongue should be a little higher in your mouth:

/ ʌ /

3 **T.2.3.B.** Listen to these pairs of words, and repeat them.

/ æ /	/ ʌ /
cap	cup
bag	bug
cat	cut
rag	rug
ankle	uncle
carry	curry
lamp	lump
paddle	puddle
hat	hut

Work with a partner. You say a word and your partner listens and points to the word he or she hears.

4 | **T.2.3.C.** | Listen to these sentences and underline all the / æ / sounds that you hear like this ___.

a. The young man was wearing fashionable sunglasses, black gloves, and a gangster's hat.
b. The wasp that's trapped in the jar of blackcurrant jam is buzzing angrily.
c. Thank you very much for coming to pay back that money you borrowed on Monday, Danny.
d. While cutting up lamb the drunken butcher hacked off his thumb with a hatchet.
e. My husband had a double brandy, my mother wanted apple juice, but I drank champagne.

Listen again and underline all the / ʌ / sounds that you hear like this 〰〰〰 .

5 Practise saying the sentences five times each. Start by saying them slowly and then say them faster and faster. Make sure you pronounce the / æ / and / ʌ / sounds correctly.

Do this exercise after the Reading on page 13 of the Student's Book.

4 The letter 'a'

The letter *a* can be pronounced in different ways. Put these words into the correct boxes.

traders	family	another	falling
donated	cracked	regular	temperature
accident	hospital	charity	after
all	disaster	happened	grateful
father	babies	danger	ligaments

/ æ /	/ eɪ /

/ ə /	/ ɑ: /

/ ɔ: /

T.2.4. Listen to the words and practise saying them.

Find some other words with *a* in the text in the Student's Book on page 13. Put them into the correct box.

● Word focus

5 -ful and -less adjectives

Adjectives from the following nouns can be formed using *-ful* or *-less*, and sometimes both.

Complete the chart.

	-ful	*-less*
pain	painful	painless
beauty		
harm		
worth		
hope		
care		
delight		
price		
help		
success		
truth		
use		
thought		
child		

T.2.5.A. Listen and practise saying all the *-ful* words. Make sure you put the stress in the correct place, and that the suffix is unstressed / fəl /.

T.2.5.B. Listen and practise saying all the *-less* words. Make sure that you stress the first syllable and that the suffix is unstressed / ləs /.

● Connected speech

6 Word linking

When a word begins with a vowel sound, and the previous word ends in a consonant, the two sounds link.

pick it up

Look at these famous book, play, and film titles and mark the linking.

War and Peace

Out of Africa

Death on the Nile

Alice in Wonderland

The Wizard of Oz

Close Encounters of the Third Kind

A CLOCKWORK ORANGE

Lawrence of Arabia

Cat on a Hot Tin Roof

Kiss of the Spiderwoman

Indiana Jones and the Temple of Doom

VENUS AND ADONIS

First among Equals

Death of a Salesman

🔲—0

T.2.6. Listen and repeat the titles, paying attention to the linking.

7 Understanding fast speech

1   T.2.7.   Listen to these Present Perfect sentences and count the number of words. *I've* counts as two words.

a. _____ post office ☐

_____ .

b. Who _____ chocolate ☐
cake?

c. _____ ☐

postcards _____
friends in England.

d. _____ ☐

English _____

_____ .

e. _____ ☐

windsurfing _____ .

f. _____ healthier _____ ☐
smoking.

g. _____ ☐

short stories _____
university.

h. _____ ☐
Transylvania?

i. What _____ hair? ☐

j. _____ half past five. ☐

🔲—0

2 Listen again and fill in the gaps.

🔲—0

Listen and follow in the tapescript. Pay attention to the pronunciation of *at*, *for*, *from*, *of*, and *to*. Are these words stressed or unstressed?

8 Prepositions – strong and weak forms

1 **T.2.8.A.** Prepositions have strong and weak forms, depending on whether they are stressed or unstressed.

Listen and repeat.

	Strong	Weak
from	/ frɒm /	/ frəm /
to	/ tu: /	/ tə / or / tʊ /
at	/ æt /	/ ət /
of	/ ɒv /	/ əv /
for	/ fɔ: /	/ fə /

2 Fill in the gaps in these sentences.
(All the prepositions are weak here.)

1. I'd like a pot _____ tea _____ breakfast, please.

2. Let's meet _____ Waterloo station _____ eight.

3. Give it _____ Julie and say it's _____ me.

4. We'll be closed on Monday because _____ the strike.

5. Elvis went _____ Las Vegas _____ four months.

T.2.8.B. Listen and check your answers.

3 Look at these sentence stress patterns and listen again. Which stress pattern goes with which sentence?

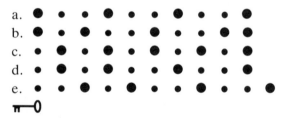

Listen again and repeat the sentences. Make sure you put the stress in the correct places, and don't forget the weak forms too.

● Stress and intonation

Do this exercise after the Listening on pages 14–15 of the Student's Book.

9 Showing definite and hesitant agreement

1 Very often, when we do not fully agree with somebody, but want to be polite, we show this in the intonation and stress patterns we use, rather than by changing the actual words.

T.2.9.A. Listen to these short exchanges between Alan, a TV producer, and Bob, a director. Bob's words **look** positive, but sometimes he agrees and sometimes he does not fully agree with Alan.

Mark Bob's replies *d* (definite agreement) or *h* (hesitant agreement), according to what you hear.

a. **A** Couldn't we tell the story from Mr Micawber's point of view?
B Yes, I suppose we could. ☐

b. **A** Couldn't we film it during the summer?
B Yes, I suppose we could. ☐

c. **A** Couldn't we film it in black and white?
B Yes, I suppose we could. ☐

d. **A** Couldn't we film it more cheaply in Hungary?
B Yes, I suppose we could. ☐

e. A Couldn't we use unknown actors in the main
    parts?
  B Yes, I suppose we could. ☐

f. A Couldn't we turn it into a musical?
  B Yes, I suppose we could. ☐

2 Look at these two sentences with the stress and
intonation marked. Which one shows definite
agreement, and which one hesitant agreement?

Yes, I suppose we could.

Yes, I suppose we could.

Listen again. This time you give Bob's replies. Use
stress and intonation to show when you agree or
don't fully agree.

3 **T.2.9.B.** In this dialogue Bob's replies have the
same certain/uncertain intonation patterns, but the
exact words are different each time. Listen and fill in
Bob's exact words.

A Didn't Harry star in a musical recently?

B Yes, _____ .

A I thought so. Wasn't it *Cats*?

B Yes, _____ .

A Now, the question is: would he be interested in
another musical so soon?

B I don't know. _____ .

A Well, is he doing anything at the National Theatre
this season?

B No, _____ .

A Right! So he'll be free next summer – just when
we need him.

B Yes, _____ .

A Hmm. Isn't Harry's nephew in the Royal
Shakespeare Company too?

B Yes, _____ .

A Well, couldn't we audition him for the part of
young David? That way we'd solve all our casting
problems.

Listen again and mark Bob's replies (d) or (h) as in 1.

4 Work with a partner. Practise reading the dialogue
aloud. Pay attention to your intonation.

● Everyday English

10 Spelling aloud

1 It is often easy to mix up these pairs of letters.

a   r   e   i   g j   s c

These letters can also be difficult.

h   k   w   x   y   z

T.2.10.A. Listen and practise saying these 14 letters
correctly.

2 **T.2.10.B.** Listen and write the words you hear spelt
out.

1. _____   9. _____
2. _____   10. _____
3. _____   11. _____
4. _____   12. _____
5. _____   13. _____
6. _____   14. _____
7. _____   15. _____
8. _____   16. _____

Work with a partner. Write eight words each using
some of the difficult letters. Take it in turns to
dictate your words, letter by letter, to your partner,
and to write down the words she/he dictates to you.
Check your spelling at the end of the exercise.

UNIT 3

● Sounds and spelling

1 The sound / ŋ / (and / n /, / ŋg /, / ndʒ /, and / ŋk /)

All Nationalities

/ ŋ /

1 **T.3.1.A.** You will hear only *one* of the three words below. Listen and circle the one that you hear.

Before you start the exercise, listen to the first three examples and make sure that you can hear the difference between the three words quite clearly.

a. (ran)	rang	rank
b. ran	(rang)	rank
c. ran	rang	(rank)
d. thin	thing	think
e. pin	ping	pink
f. win	wing	wink
g. sin	sing	sink
h. sun	sung	sunk
i. bun	bung	bunk
j. banner	banger	banker

🔑—0

2 Practise making the sounds / n / and / ŋ /. To make the sound / ŋ / the air should come out through your nose, as in the sound / n /. But your tongue should go up towards the *back* of your mouth, *not* the front:

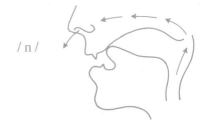

/ n /

Listen again and repeat the words. Make sure that the difference between the sounds / n / and / ŋ / is clear, and that you do *not* add a / g / or / k / to the words ending in / ŋ /.

3 Look back at the groups of words above. Working with a partner, say one of the words and get your partner to point to the word that you have just said.

4 Work in pairs. Put the sentences below into the correct order. There may be more than one possibility.

   a. skating rink/Aunt Angela/at a/a tango/Uncle Frank/Birmingham/with/while dancing/banged/her ankle/.
   b. at the pretty, young singer/in a singles' bar/winked/drinking/the Hong Kong gangster/singing romantic songs/a gin sling/.
   c. tongue/pink/long/thing/stringy/what's/Angus King's/that/on/?
   d. hanged/for killing/a boxing ring/wrongfully/a Singapore dancer/Washington banker/outside/was/a/.

   T.3.1.B. Listen and compare your answers to the tape.

Listen again and underline ___ any words spelt with *ng* where the *g* is pronounced (/ g /).

🔑—0

Practise saying the sentences correctly.

14

5 Put the following words into the correct box below, according to the pronunciation of -*nger*.

singer	plunger	coathanger	bellringer
anger	ironmonger	hunger	danger
stranger	challenger	left-winger	ginger
banger	finger	linger	

/ ŋə /	/ ŋgə /
singer	*anger*

/ ndʒə /
stranger

T.3.1.C. Listen and check your answers.
π—0

Listen again and practise saying the words correctly.

---

2 The sound / r /
(All Nationalities)

1 T.3.2.A. Below are ten adjectives that describe personal characteristics. Can you remember what they all mean?

You will hear them read in British and American accents. Listen to each word in both accents and mark them like this ✓ if *r* is pronounced and ✗ if it is not.

British	American
a. ha~~r~~dwo~~r~~king	hardworking ✓ ✓
b. reliable	reliable
c. practical	practical
d. sincere	sincere
e. organized	organized
f. proud	proud
g. relaxed	relaxed
h. careless	careless
i. popular	popular

2 Answer the following questions:

When *r* comes *before* the vowel sound in the syllable is it pronounced in

a. American English? _____

b. British English? _____

When *r* comes *after* the vowel sound in the syllable is it pronounced in

a. American English? _____

b. British English? _____
π—0

3 How do you think the following adjectives are pronounced in British English?

extrovert	warm-hearted
superior	self-centred
cheerful	good-natured
particular	short-tempered

T.3.2.B. Listen to see if you guessed correctly.

4 Practise the sound / r /. You should turn up the tip of your tongue, like this:

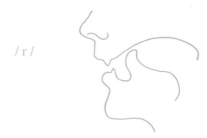

/ r /

The tip of your tongue should **not** touch the roof of your mouth, and your tongue should **not** vibrate.

Practise saying the adjectives in 1. You can say them in either the British or American way, but make sure that you pronounce / r / correctly.

● Word focus

Do this exercise after the questionnaire on pages 22–3 of the Student's Book.

3 Words ending in -ion

1 Most of the words below come from the job questionnaire in the Student's Book. Can you remember what they all mean?

Before you listen, try to guess where the stress is in each of these words.

profession	promotion	instruction
fashion	conclusion	occupation
question	completion	emotion
solution	option	communication

T.3.3.A. Listen and see if you guessed correctly.

What do you notice about the position of the stress? How is -ion pronounced in English?

2 Listen again and practise saying the words correctly. If you have problems, try starting with the stressed syllable, like this:

●	●
pation	cation
cupation	nication
occupation	munication
	communication

3 The vowel sound in the stressed syllable of these words often causes problems. Sometimes it has a short sound / æ /, / e /, / ɒ / or / ʌ /. Sometimes it has a long sound / eɪ /, / iː /, / əʊ / or / uː /.

Put the words in 1 opposite into the following table according to the pronunciation of the vowel sound in the stressed syllable.

short	long
a	
/ æ /	/ eɪ /

short	long
e	
/ e /	/ iː /
profession	

short	long
o	
/ ɒ /	/ əʊ /
	promotion

short	long
u	
/ ʌ /	/ juː / or / uː /

Can you see any pattern? Look at the number of consonants between the stressed vowel and the suffix -ion.

4 Work out the pronunciation of the following words.

consumption	deduction	fraction
passion	explosion	inspection
devotion	adoption	lotion
reception	confusion	inflation
persuasion	completion	contribution
protection		

T.3.3.B. Listen to see if you are correct.

Listen again and practise saying the words correctly.

4 Job vocabulary – revision

Below are fourteen words related to work. Can you transcribe them from phonemic script? Can you remember what they all mean?

1. /ˈpeɪ raɪz/ *pay rise*   (n.)

2. /ˈsæləri/ _____

3. /æplɪˈkeɪʃn/ _____

4. /kəˈrɪə/ _____

5. /sæk/ _____

6. /dɪˈɡriː/ _____

7. /rɪˈtaɪə/ _____

8. /prəˈməʊʃn/ _____

9. /ˈəʊvətaɪm/ _____

10. /ʃɪfts/ _____

11. /ˈweɪdʒɪz/ _____

12. /ˈtreɪnɪŋ/ _____

13. /ˈkwɒlɪfaɪd/ _____

14. /rɪˈdʌndənt/ _____

T.3.4. With a partner decide exactly how they are pronounced. Listen and check to see if you transcribed them correctly.

Write next to the words (n.) if they are nouns, (v.) if they are verbs and (a.) if they are adjectives. Do you know any more words in the same word families?

π—0

● Connected speech

5 English punctuation marks and dictation

1 Write the names of these punctuation marks in the spaces.

a. , _____

b. . _____

c. ? _____

d. ! _____

e : _____

f. ; _____

g. ' _____

h. ' ' _____

i. — _____

j. —— _____

T.3.5.A. Listen and check your answers.

π—0

2 **T.3.5.B.** You will now hear a passage about two women – Alice and Cynthia. Listen to the whole passage and concentrate on the meaning of what you hear. Which woman enjoys her job? Why?

T.3.5.C. Listen again. This time you will hear the passage broken into short phrases marked by a tone. When you hear the tone, stop the tape and write down the phrases you hear, taking care with punctuation.

T.3.5.D. Listen again. This time you will hear the passage broken into sentences. Check what you have written, paying attention to spelling and punctuation.

π—0

6 Linking 'r'

1 Even in British English, the *r* at the end of a word or syllable is sometimes pronounced.

T.3.6.A. Listen to the adjectives below and say when the *r* in *over-* is pronounced and when it is **not**.

> over-ambitious   over-organized
> over-careful   over-excited
> over-qualified   over-paid
> over-intellectual over-modest
> over-confident   over-educated

Listen again and practise saying them correctly.

2 Can you understand the special meaning of *over-*... in each case? Work with a partner. Describe what these words mean.

Examples
Being over-modest is when you're so modest that you're not really honest about your achievements.
If a person is over-paid, then they get more money than they deserve.

3 **T.3.6.B.** Listen to the following short dialogue between Margaret and Peter. Mark the linking *r* sounds.

M Peter! Are you going anywhere over Easter this year?
P Well, yes, as a matter of fact we are. We're off on tour of Italy for a week or two.
M Mmm. That sounds really wonderful. Where exactly will you be going?
P Oh, here and there. Rome's more or less definite, but apart from that we're open to suggestion.
M Are you travelling by coach?
P No, by car, actually.
M Dear old Italy! When you're in Rome you must remember to throw a coin over your shoulder into the Trevi fountain.
P Really? What for?
M Well, if you do that, it means that, sooner or later, you're sure to return.

Work in pairs. Read the dialogue aloud, paying attention to the *r* sounds.

● Stress and intonation

7 Contrastive stress

1 **T.3.7.** Listen to the dialogues below and mark the **main stress** in **B's** answer like this ■.

a. **A** Is your mother going to California?
   B No, my mother's g■one to California.

b. **A** Has your mother gone to New York?
   B No, my mother's gone to California■.

c. **A** Has your father gone to California?
   B No, my mother's gone to California.

d. **A** Has Jane's mother gone to California?
   B No, my mother's gone to California.

2 Why is a different word stressed in each answer?
π—0

3 Listen again and repeat the answers and then practise reading the dialogues with a partner.

4 Here are some more groups of answers with the stress in various places. Try to write a question for each answer.

a. _____ ?

   No, I've ■lost fifty pounds.

   _____ ?

   No, I've lost ■fifty pounds.

   _____ ?

   No, I've lost fifty■ pounds.

   _____ ?

   No, ■I've lost fifty pounds.

b. _____ ?

No, my sister's broken her leg.

_____ ?

No, my sister's broken her leg.

_____ ?

No, my sister's broken her leg.

_____ ?

No, my sister's broken her leg.

c. _____ ?

No, the Baileys have bought a flat in London.

_____ ?

No, the Baileys have bought a flat in London.

_____ ?

No, the Baileys have bought a flat in London.

_____ ?

No, the Baileys have bought a flat in London.

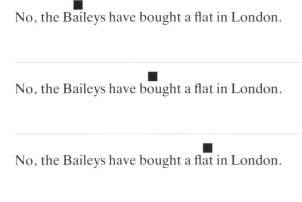

(Possible answers)

5 Practise reading your dialogues with a partner.

---

8 Main stress with *So do I*, etc.

1 **T.3.8.A.** A group of teenagers is discussing their future. Listen and fill in the missing words.

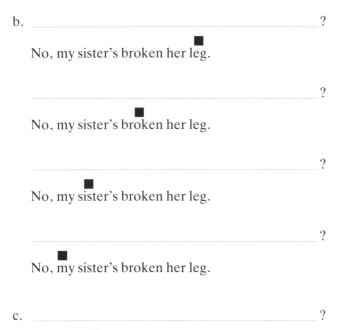

2 Listen again and mark the answers *a* if they agree with the first speaker and *d* if they disagree with him or her, like this:

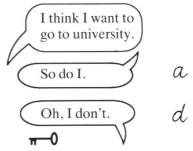

3 Which word is the most stressed in **all** of these answers? Why? What happens to the auxiliary verbs *do*, *have*, and *can* when they come before the pronoun?

Listen and repeat the short answers, paying attention to the stress and weak forms.

4 **T.3.8.B.** Listen to **A** and **B** talking about their work lives and qualifications. You take the part of **C**, either agreeing or disagreeing as the case may be, like this:

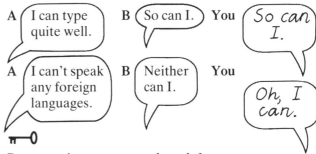

Pay attention to stress and weak forms.

Write eight more statements about your own work life. Read them to a partner who can decide whether or not they are true for him/her.

9 Showing interest – short questions

1   Look at the short dialogues below and fill in speaker **B's** part, as in the example.

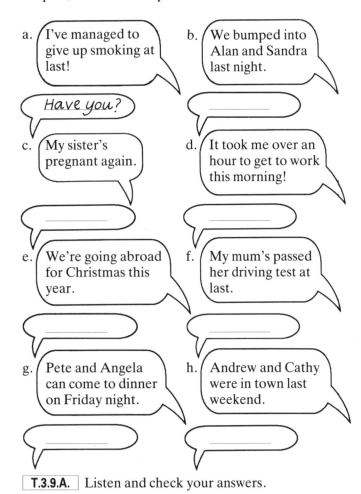

a. I've managed to give up smoking at last!

Have you?

b. We bumped into Alan and Sandra last night.

_____

c. My sister's pregnant again.

_____

d. It took me over an hour to get to work this morning!

_____

e. We're going abroad for Christmas this year.

_____

f. My mum's passed her driving test at last.

_____

g. Pete and Angela can come to dinner on Friday night.

_____

h. Andrew and Cathy were in town last weekend.

_____

T.3.9.A.   Listen and check your answers.

2   In four of the dialogues, speaker **B** sounds **interested** in what speaker **A** is saying, in four of them he **doesn't**. Listen again and mark them *I* if he sounds interested and *U* if he sounds uninterested.

3   Practise the short questions sounding interested. Your voice should start **low** and rise. To practise you can try exaggerating at first, like this:

Have you? .... Have you? .... Have you?

4   T.3.9.B.   Listen and take the part of **B**. You should respond with similar short questions. Make sure that your intonation sounds **interested**.

Diana's got a new job.   *Has she?*   Has she?

You listen   *You speak*   *You listen*

● Everyday English

10 Jobs with international names

1   Look at the jobs below. Are the same or similar words used in your language? If not, make sure you know what the jobs are.

T.3.10   Listen and mark the stress on each word.

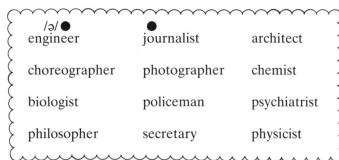

/ə/●	●	
engineer	journalist	architect
choreographer	photographer	chemist
biologist	policeman	psychiatrist
philosopher	secretary	physicist

Mark the / ə / sounds.

Listen again and practise saying the words correctly.

2   Work with a partner and discuss the answers to the questions below:

a. Which of these people might work in a laboratory?
b. Which of these people work with numbers a lot?
c. Which of these jobs most involve working with people?
d. Which of these people need a lot of imagination, do you think?
e. For which of these jobs do you **not** need a degree?
f. Which ones do you think you might enjoy doing, if you were properly qualified?
g. Which do you think you would really hate doing?

UNIT 4

● Sounds and spelling

Do this before the Controlled Practice exercises on page 37 of the Student's Book.

1 The sounds / v / and / w /
Ⓓ Ⓗ Ⓙ Ⓣⓡ

1 | T.4.1.A. | Listen and circle the words you hear.

  a. veal   wheel
  b. veils   whales
  c. vine   wine
  d. vest   west
  e. viper   wiper

2 Practise making the sounds.

To make the sound / v / your top teeth should touch the inside of your bottom lip like this:

/ v /

To make the sound / w / your teeth don't touch your lips. Your lips should be hard and round like this:

/ w /

If you have problems with the sound / w / you can try starting with / u: / like this:

uuu → why
 uu → why
  u → why

3 | T.4.1.B. | Listen to these words, and repeat them.

/ v /	/ w /
veal	wheel
veils	whales
vine	wine
vest	west
viper	wiper
verse	worse
vet	wet

4 | T.4.1.C. | Listen and fill in the boxes.

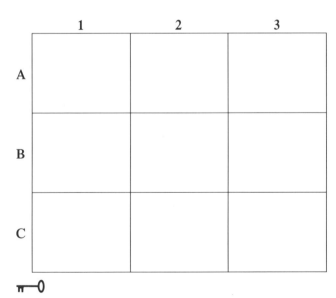

5 Work with a partner. Without letting your partner see, fill the grid marked *You* with nine / w / and / v / words. Remember you can use a word more than once. Now one of you dictate what you have written so that the other can write it down in the box in the grid marked *Your partner*.

	1	2	3
A			
B			
C			

You

	1	2	3
A			
B			
C			

Your partner

Example
A What is in box A1?
B West.
A And in box B1?
B Er . . . veal.

Do this before the Controlled Practice exercises on page 37 of the Student's Book.

2 Silent letter '*w*'

1 Fill in the crossword. All the words have a silent *w*.

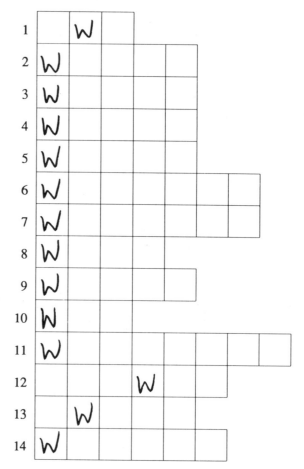

Clues
1. One and one
2. Ankle is to foot as .... is to hand
3. Two halves make a ....
4. Not right
5. The Titantic is a very famous ....
6. A line on the face is called a ....
7. Worms .... when they move
8. People often .... presents up in coloured paper before they give them
9. Put words on paper
10. .... starts a question about someone
11. Fighter who tries to throw someone to the ground without hitting them
12. Reply to a question
13. Long metal blade used as a weapon
14. Circle of flowers to put on someone's grave

2 | T.4.2. | Now listen and repeat. Take care **not** to sound the *w* in each word.

3 Complete the rule:

When *w* comes before the letter _____ or the

letters _____ it is silent. The words _____ ,

_____ , and _____ also have silent *ws*.

π—0

Do this before the Reading on pages 30–2 of the Student's Book.

3 Silent letter '*g*'

1 In some of these words the *g* is sounded. In some it is silent. Put them in the correct column.

gnome	gnat	resign
sign	ignition	foreign
dignified	reign	signature
gnaw	recognition	ignorance
resignation	ignore	campaign
ignite	foreigner	significance

Sounded *g*	Silent *g*
ignition	*gnome*

π—0

2 | T.4.3. | Listen and practise saying the words with sounded *g* and the words with silent *g*.

3 Complete the rule:

When the letters *gn* come at the _____ or the

_____ of a word *g* is silent. Some other words, like

_____ for example, also contain silent *g*.

π—0

● Word focus

Do this after the Reading on pages 30–2 of the Student's Book.

4 Opposites with *in-*, *im-*, *ir-*, and *il-*

1 To make opposites we often use the prefixes *in-*, *im-*, *ir-*, and *il-*.

What are the opposites of these adjectives?

1. effective _____
2. direct _____
3. polite _____
4. curable _____
5. significant _____
6. rational _____
7. mature _____
8. formal _____
9. legal _____
10. regular _____
11. logical _____
12. moral _____
13. correct _____
14. perfect _____
15. responsible _____
16. sufficient _____

π—0

2 Complete the rules:

We use *im-* + words beginning with the letters _____

or _____ .

We use *ir-* + words beginning with the letter _____ .

We use *il-* + words beginning with the letter _____ .

π—0

3 Put the negative adjectives into the correct box according to stress.

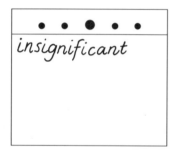

• • •	• • ●
informal	indirect

• ● • •	• • ● •
incurable	ineffective

• • ● • •
insignificant

4 **T.4.4.** Listen and check your answers.

5 Listen again and practise saying the words with the correct stress.

6 Write sentences to show the meaning of five negative adjectives.

Examples
He's suffering from an *incurable* skin disease. The doctors say there's nothing they can do for him.

It's going to be quite an *informal* party, so there's no need to dress up.

7 Work in pairs.

Student A Read out your example sentences, but say 'inkblot' each time, instead of the negative adjectives.

Example: He's suffering from an *inkblot* skin disease. The doctors say there's nothing they can do for him.

Student B Listen and guess the negative adjectives each time.

5 Vocabulary of literature

1 Look at the phonemic transcriptions and write the words. All of them are related to either prose writing, poetry, or drama.

a. / ˈtʃæptə / _____

b. / raɪm / _____

c. / ˈkærəktə / _____

d. / ˈhɪərəʊ / _____

e. / siːn / _____

f. / ˈɔːθə / _____

g. / ˈrɪðəm / _____

h. / ˈherəʊɪn / _____

i. / ˈdaɪəlɒg / _____

j. / ˈpleɪraɪt / _____

k. / ˈsaɪəns ˈfɪkʃn / _____

l. / nəˈreɪtə / _____

m. / ˈhɒrə ˈstɔːrɪ / _____

n. / ˈpəʊɪm / _____

o. / ˌɔː təbaɪ ˈɒgrəfɪ / _____

p. / ˈpəʊɪt / _____

π—O

T.4.5. Listen and practise saying the words. Look at the phonemic transcript as you say each one.

2 The following sentences have some mistakes in them. Can you correct them?

a. Hans Andersen wrote some wonderful science fiction stories.
b. The hero of the book is a girl called Alice.
c. Anthony Burgess's autobiography of Shakespeare is an interesting book.
d. Oscar Wilde was the narrator of *The Picture of Dorian Gray*.
e. The last chapter of the opera—when Mimi dies in front of her helpless friends—always brings tears to my eyes.
f. *Venus and Adonis* is a famous rhyme by Shakespeare.
g. The conversation in Oscar Wilde's plays is always very good.
h. Mickey Mouse is a very famous cartoon hero.

π—O

(Possible answers)

● Connected speech

Do this after exercise 4 on page 37 of the Student's Book.

6 Prepositions – strong or weak forms?

1 **T.4.6.A.** Look at these sentences. Listen and repeat.

I'm from London.
I spoke to Tom.
I'm waiting for Frank.
It's made of plastic.
It's on at 8.30.

2 **T.4.6.B.** Look at these questions. Listen and repeat.

What's it made of?
Who did you speak to?
What time's it on at?
Where are you from?
Who are you waiting for?

3 What do you notice about the prepositions in the sentences and in the questions? Why is the pronunciation different?

4 Listen to the questions again. This time reply, using the words in boxes. Make sure you pronounce the prepositions correctly.

a.	plastic leather	wood glass	rubber metal

b.	Tom Tracy	Terry Jane	Pat Jim

c.	8.30 10.25	4.20 9 o'clock	midnight 6.35

d.	London Istanbul	Madrid Paris	Rome Munich

e.	Frank George	Philip Mike	Sue Carol

5 Work with a partner. Choose one of these objects. Your partner must guess which object you are thinking of by asking questions like this:

A What's it made of?
B It's made of metal.
A What's it used for?
B It's used for watering flowers.

● Stress and intonation

Do this after exercises 5–7 on page 37–8 of the Student's Book.

7 Asking questions indirectly

1 Ask the following questions indirectly.

a. Who wrote *The French Lieutenant's Woman*?

Can you tell me *who wrote The French Lieutenant's Woman* ?

b. When was it written?

Have you got any idea _____ ?

c. Has *The Magus* ever been made into a film?

Do you happen to know _____

_____ ?

d. Who are the main characters in the book?

Do you know _____

_____ ?

2 **T.4.7.** Listen to these questions which are asked indirectly. Does the intonation rise or fall at the end? Is the intonation pattern always the same?

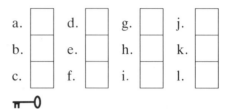

3 Listen again and repeat the questions. Make sure that your intonation is correct.

4 Write six questions like these about some of the books below.

Example
Do you know who wrote *Don Quixote*?

The Picture of Dorian Gray	*Dr Zhivago*
Murder on the Orient Express	*Dracula*
Dr Jekyll and Mr Hyde	*Don Quixote*
A Clockwork Orange	*Moby Dick*
The Name of the Rose	*Candide*
The Tragedy of Man	*1984*
The Invisible Man	*Out of Africa*
Death in Venice	

Ask your questions to your classmates.

Example
A Have you got any idea who wrote *Out of Africa*?
B No, I'm afraid I haven't.
C Yes, wasn't it Karen Blixen?

Do this after exercise 8 on page 38 of the Student's Book.

8 Tag questions

1 Write the tag questions for these sentences.

a. He's an astrologer, _____?

b. You don't believe in ghosts, _____?

c. That can't be a true story, _____?

d. You've seen *The Exorcist*, _____?

e. You wouldn't scream, _____?

f. She's got a black cat, _____?

g. There wasn't a strange smell in the room,

_____?

h. Nobody spoke, _____?

i. It was a UFO, _____?

j. She's afraid of the dark, _____?

k. You'd never walk under a ladder, _____?

l. He can bend forks by willpower, _____?

2 **T.4.8.A.** Listen to the tag questions. Do they rise or fall? Write R or F according to what you hear.

a.		d.		g.		j.	
b.		e.		h.		k.	
c.		f.		i.		l.	

3 Sometimes it can be difficult to hear the rises and falls clearly. Here are some rules to guide you.

a. The voice pitch **drops** before a rise:

Ghosts don't exist, do they?

b. The voice pitch **goes up** before a fall:

You've never seen one, have you?

T.4.8.B. Listen to these up and down tag questions and repeat them. You can practise the intonation by first exaggerating.

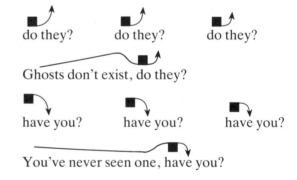

4 Look at the words below. Do you know what they mean? Write the ones you know in the first column on the next page, and the ones that you don't know in the second column.

astrology	kleptomania	vertigo
phrenology	philately	ornithology
claustrophobia	agoraphobia	graphology
entomology	bibliophile	etymology

I know what it means	I'm not sure what it means

5 Write short definitions of the words you know.

Example
Astrology means using the stars to predict the future.

For words that you're not sure of, write what you think they may mean. (Use your imagination. Don't use a dictionary!)

6 Read out your definitions – real and imaginary – to a partner. Use **down** tag questions for those words **you're sure of**, and **up** tag questions for those words **you're unsure of**.

Astrology means using the stars to predict the future,

doesn't it?   or   doesn't it?

Your partner should listen and say if you're sure or unsure.

7 When you've finished, check the meaning of the words you don't know.

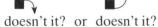

● **Everyday English**

Do this after the Discussion point on pages 29–30 of the Student's Book.

9 Saying horoscope signs

1 In English we use Latin names for the twelve horoscope signs.

Aries *21 March–20 April*	**Libra** *24 Sept–23 Oct*
Aquarius *21 Jan–19 Feb*	**Pisces** *20 Feb–20 March*
Cancer *22 June–23 July*	**Sagittarius** *23 Nov–21 Dec*
Capricorn *22 Dec–20 Jan*	**Scorpio** *24 Oct–22 Nov*
Gemini *22 May–21 June*	**Taurus** *21 April–21 May*
Leo *24 July–23 Aug*	**Virgo** *24 Aug–23 Sept*

Can you write the correct Latin names next to the pictures?

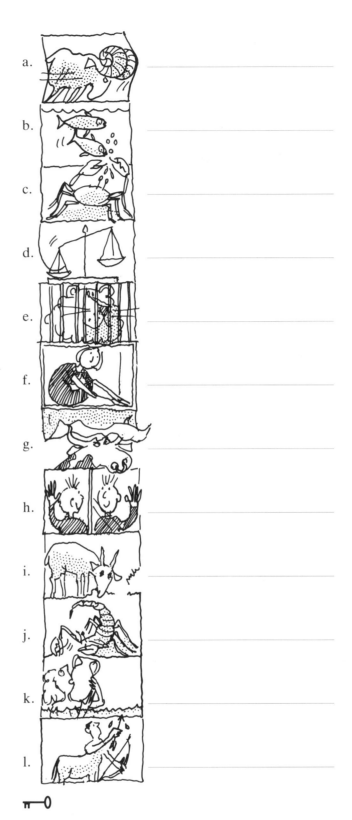

a. _____

b. _____

c. _____

d. _____

e. _____

f. _____

g. _____

h. _____

i. _____

j. _____

k. _____

l. _____

2 **T.4.9.** Listen and repeat. Make sure you stress the words correctly.

3 What sign are you? What about your classmates, colleagues, and members of your family? Are there any similarities between people who are born under the same star sign? What are they?

Discuss your views with a partner.

UNIT 5

● Sounds and spelling

1 The sounds / θ /, / t /, and / s /
Ⓓ Ⓔ Ⓕ Ⓖⓡ Ⓗ Ⓘ Ⓙ Ⓟ

1 **T.5.1.A.** The sound / θ / is often pronounced wrongly – as / t / or / s /. Listen and make sure that you can hear the difference between the three sounds:

/ θ /	/ t /	/ s /
theme	team	seem

2 **T.5.1.B.** Below are groups of three words. On the tape you will hear **four** words. Listen and circle the one that you hear **twice**.

a.	thin	sin	tin
b.	thank	sank	tank
c.	thick	sick	tick
d.	thigh	sigh	tie
e.	path	pass	part
f.	thought	sort	taught
g.	tenth	tense	tent
h.	faith	face	fate
i.	fourth	force	fought

🗝—0

3 Notice the different position of the tongue when making these three sounds. The sound / t / is made **further back** in the mouth than in most languages:

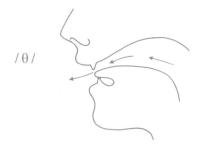

/ θ /

a.

/ t /

b.

/ s /

If you have problems with the sound / θ /, try putting your finger in front of your mouth and touching it with your tongue like this:

/ θ /

4 Listen and repeat the words above, making sure that the difference between them is clear.

28

5 | T.5.1.C. | Listen to the following dialogue between Simon and Sally. Underline the words you think will be difficult to say.

Simon Sally, have you got anything planned for Thursday?
Sally For Thursday, Simon?
Simon For Thursday the 13th. It's my birthday, you see.
Sally Simon! Your birthday! Thank heavens you said!
Simon Yes, I'm going to be thirty-three. I thought I'd throw a party or something to celebrate.
Sally What a super idea!
Simon Do you think you'll be free?
Sally For Thursday? Yes, I think so.
Simon Fine, so I'll see you soon. It starts at six.
Sally Yes. Thanks . . . oh, and Simon . . .
Simon Yes?
Sally Sorry I'm so slow.

6 Practise saying the words you've underlined.

Work with a partner and read the dialogue aloud. Make sure you pronounce all the / θ / sounds correctly.

7 On a piece of paper write eight of the *thin/sin/tin* words. Dictate them to your partner and then compare your lists. Have you both written the same words?

---

2 The sounds / ð /, / d /, and / z /
Ⓓ Ⓔ Ⓕ ⒢ᵣ Ⓗ Ⓘ Ⓙ Ⓟ

1 | T.5.2.A. | Listen to the first word on each of the cards below.

/ ð /

then	with	breathe
there	they	southern
loathe	those	clothing

/ d /

den	dare	lied
sudden	day	she'd
tide	breed	load

/ z /

Zen	whizz	she's
lies	lose	breeze
doze	closing	ties

Can you hear the difference between the sounds / z /, / d /, and / ð /?

2 | T.5.2.B. | Now listen and cross out the words that you hear on the tape, like this:

You will hear each word twice.

Which is the first card to have all the words crossed out? Which is the second?

3 Notice the different positions of the tongue in these three sounds. The sound / d / is made **further back** in the mouth in English than in many languages.

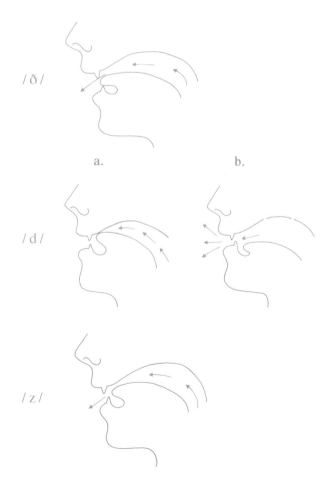

Notice that all three sounds are **voiced**.

29

If you have problems with the sound / ð / try putting your finger in front of your mouth and touching it with your tongue, in the same way as with the sound / θ /.

/ ð /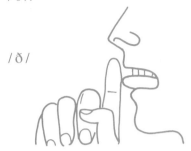

4 **Bingo**

Work in groups of five or six. One person in the group should be the caller. This person does not need to fill in the card below. The others should fill it in with **any** nine words in 1 above.

The caller should read out the words from 1 above in whatever order he/she wants, putting a cross (x) next to the words read out as a memory check. The others should listen and cross out the words that they hear. The first person to cross out all the words should shout 'Bingo!'. Then the winner should show his/her card to check that the words on it are words the caller has marked.

3 Practising the sounds / θ /, / ð /, / t /, / d /, / s /, and / z / together

1 Read the dialogue below. When you think the letters *th* are pronounced / θ / underline them like this ___ . When you think the letters *th* are pronounced / ð / underline them like this ∿ .

2 ⬚ **T.5.3.** ⬚ Listen and check to see if you were right.

A How are Judith and Timothy Thorpe's triplets?
B Those three? Well . . . both Heather and Cathy are very healthy, but I think they're having rather a lot of trouble with Matthew.
A With Matthew? What's the matter with Matthew?
B Teething troubles, I think, and then he won't eat anything.
A Teething troubles? But how old are the triplets now?
B I think they're about thirteen months.
A Thirteen months? Oh, I thought they were a lot younger than that.
B No, they must be thirteen months because it was their first birthday at the end of last month – on the thirtieth . . . or was it the thirty-first?
A Oh, dear, and I didn't send them anything, not even a birthday card . . . I wonder what Judith and Timothy thought?
B Don't distress yourself dear, they didn't say anything to me . . .

π—0

3 Listen again and repeat the dialogue in short sections. Pay attention to your pronunciation of the sounds / t /, / d /, / s /, / z /, / θ /, and / ð /.

4 Practise reading the dialogue with a partner.

5 On the tape the first woman is a little nervous and the second is quite sympathetic. Try reading the dialogue again with your partner, but this time make the first woman **very** nervous and the second woman very **un**sympathetic.

● Word focus

Do this exercise after the section on homophones on page 42 of the Student's Book.

4 Homophones

1 There are two possible words for each phonemic transcription below. Can you find them?

a. /sʌn/   *sun*   *son*

b. /pɑ:st/ _____ _____

c. /feə/ _____ _____

d. /beə/ _____ _____

e. /ə'laʊd/ _____ _____

f. /swi:t/ _____ _____

π—0

2   T.5.4.   Listen to the following sentences and short dialogues. They all sound correct, but each one contains a word which is spelt wrongly. Underline these homophones and write the correct spelling in the spaces provided.

a. <u>Witch</u> channel is *My Fair Lady* on?   *Which*

b. I don't know weather to go to the pool or not.

_____

c. Who's watch is this on the floor? _____

d. He used to be a kernel in the army. _____

e. The dog wagged its tale happily. _____

f. A Is he one of the town councillors?

   B No, he's the mare of the town. _____

g. I practice playing the guitar every day. _____

h. Most of the gorillas were armed with machine

   guns and hand grenades. _____

i. Brrr . . . Close the window! There's a terrible

   draft in here. _____

j. The lion gave a loud raw and then ran off. _____

π—0

Use a dictionary to check the meaning of any new words.

● Connected speech

5 Hearing the difference between past and present tenses

1   T.5.5.   Sometimes when people are speaking very quickly, it is difficult to hear the difference between past and present tenses. Listen to these sentences and write *past* if a Past Simple, Past Continuous or Past Perfect tense is used. Write *present* if a Present or Present Perfect tense is used.

a. _____   f. _____

b. _____   g. _____

c. _____   h. _____

d. _____   i. _____

e. _____   j. _____

π—0

2 Why is it sometimes difficult to hear the difference between past and present tenses?

π—0

3 Listen again and repeat the sentences, paying attention to the weak forms of auxiliaries, and to word linking.

6 Linking with common expressions

1 In fast speech, consonants at the end of words often link on to the next word, if the next word starts with a vowel:

Watch out!   Come on!   What's up?

2 How do you think the following expressions are pronounced when they are said quickly?

SHUT UP   *Come in*   **Come on**

Watch out   **Hold on**

Get out   *Forget it*   Look out

What's up   WAKE UP   Pick it up

WAIT A MINUTE   Have a nice time

   T.5.6.A.   Listen and practise saying them.

3 **T.5.6.B.** The expressions below link together in a different way when they are said quickly. What is the rule for each group? Listen and decide.

A B C

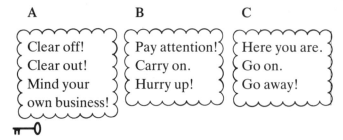

Clear off!
Clear out!
Mind your own business!

Pay attention!
Carry on.
Hurry up!

Here you are.
Go on.
Go away!

🔑—0

Listen again and practise saying them quickly.

4 Look at these expressions:

Nex~~t~~ please!   Please~~d~~ to meet you!

In fast speech, the letters *t* and *d* at the end of words are often silent when the next word starts with a consonant.

5 **T.5.6.C.** Listen to the following expressions and practise saying them.

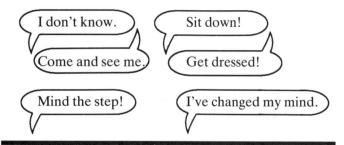

I don't know.
Come and see me.

Sit down!
Get dressed!

Mind the step!

I've changed my mind.

7 Reading aloud

1 **T.5.7.A.** Listen to the following reading passage. Read the text silently as you listen.

'Anywhere special you want to sit?' Mr White asked.

'It's all the same to me,' answered Mr Green. 'It won't be for long, anyhow.'

The two men made their way up to the front of the carriage, and sat down together in the seat just behind the driver's cab. There were plenty of empty seats; Mr White's question had evidently been a sign that he was accepting, thus early in the evening, the role of host. Since he was taking his friend home to dinner at his house, he wished to assume responsibility for his comfort straightaway, as soon as they boarded the train. Mr Green lived on the other side of Manchester, and usually went home from the office by bus; so that, in a sense, the train was already foreign ground to him, and home ground to Mr White.

Recognizing this situation, Mr Green volunteered, 'Makes a big difference, doesn't it? Having them electrified.'

'All the difference in the world,' said Mr White.

The driver, who had been leaning out of his window conversing with a man on the platform, settled into his seat. The train started.

'Smooth,' said Mr Green.

'Makes a very easy journey of it,' said Mr White. They might have been discussing some fitting in Mr White's own house.

2 **T.5.7.B.** You will now hear the same passage broken up into short phrases. Listen and repeat each phrase, paying attention to word linking and to intonation.

3 **T.5.7.C.** You will now hear the same passage broken up into longer sentences. Listen and repeat each sentence, paying attention to intonation and phrasing.

4 Now read the whole passage through aloud, paying attention to phrasing and to pace.

● Stress and intonation

Do this exercise after looking at the expressions on page 46 of the Student's Book.

8 Intonation with common expressions

1 **T.5.8.A.** Listen to the dialogues below and write in what **B** says.

a. Jack and I have decided to get married.

b. We lost our tennis match.

c. To our health!

d. See you later, Mark.

e. Auntie Margaret's very ill again.

f. I'm just going to ask my bank manager for a loan.

g. See you on Monday.

h. We're going to Karen's party now, Mum.

2 Listen again and repeat **B's** part, paying attention to the intonation. Remember that if your intonation is very flat you may sound bored or unsympathetic.

3 **T.5.8.B.** Now listen to the people on the tape and respond with an appropriate expression. There may be more than one possibility.

● Everyday English

9 Signs at airports and railway stations

1 Here are some signs that you might see at an airport or railway station. Do you know what they all mean?

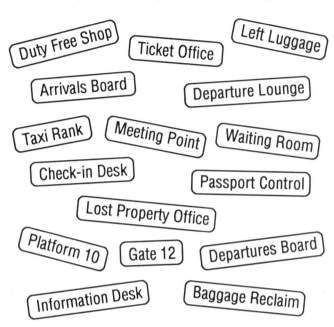

Duty Free Shop · Ticket Office · Left Luggage · Arrivals Board · Departure Lounge · Taxi Rank · Meeting Point · Waiting Room · Check-in Desk · Passport Control · Lost Property Office · Platform 10 · Gate 12 · Departures Board · Information Desk · Baggage Reclaim

2 Put them into the correct box, according to where you might find them.

A Airport

B Railway Station

C Both

3   **T.5.9.**   Listen and check your answers.

4   Listen again. Which words are stressed? Mark the
     main stresses and secondary stresses, like this:

     •   ●   •
     duty free shop

     Practise saying the words correctly.

5   Which of these places might you go to if you were
     leaving from a railway station? What about if you
     were leaving from an airport?

     Which places might you go to after getting off a
     train? What about after getting off a plane?

6   Working with a partner, practise some short
     dialogues at either an airport or a railway station,
     like this:

     A Excuse me, do you happen to know where *the
     duty free shop* is?
     B Yes, it's just round the corner on your left.
               or
     A Is this the right way for *left luggage*?
     B I'm afraid I don't know.

10 Saying centuries

1   **T.5.10.A.** It is often very difficult to remember
     dates. Use the clues on the tape to try and decide
     which of the dates on the right answer the questions
     on the left.

     Remember
     1900–1932 is the **beginning** of the 20th century
     1933–1966 is the **middle** of the 20th century
     1967–1999 is the **end** of the 20th century
     100–1 BC is the **first** century BC
     200–101 BC is the **second** century BC
     300–201 BC is the **third** century BC

a. When did Christopher Columbus discover America?	429 BC
b. When did Julius Caesar die?	1715
c. When did Catherine the Great become Empress of Russia?	44 BC
d. When did Henry VIII become King of England?	1492
e. When was Plato born?	1804
f. When did Louis XIV die?	1509
g. When did Napoleon become Emperor of France?	1762
h. When did Alexander the Great die?	323 BC

2   Listen to the clues again and practise saying them.

3   **T.5.10.B.** Now respond to the questions on the tape
     like this:

     Example

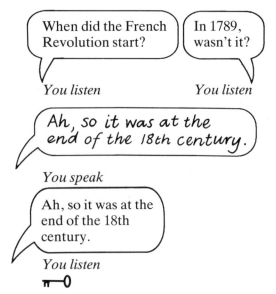

UNIT 6

● Sounds and spelling

1 The sounds / ɒ /, / ɔ: /, and / əʊ /
(All Nationalities)

1 **T.6.1.A.** Listen to the following three names. Make sure you can hear the difference between the vowel sounds.

/ ɒ /
1. Rob

/ ɔ: /
2. Dawn

/ əʊ /
3. Joan

2 **T.6.1.B.** Listen to the following items of food and put them on the correct shopping list according to the vowel sound underlined.

r**o**lls	w**a**lnuts	c**o**c**oa**	av**o**cad**o**s
ch**o**ps	c**au**liflower	c**o**ffee	sweetc**o**rn
pr**a**wns	y**o**ghurt	**o**ranges	c**o**ke
lobster	pot**a**t**oe**s	macar**o**ni	strawberries
s**au**sages	ch**o**colate	c**ou**rgettes	**au**bergines

Rob's list / ɒ /

chops

Dawn's list / ɔ: /

prawns

Joan's list / əʊ /

rolls

T.6.1.C. Who has got the longest list? Whose list is the shortest? Listen and check.

35

3 Practise making the three sounds:

a. The sound / ɒ / is a short sound. It is made at the **back** of the mouth with the tongue **down**. Your lips should look like this when you make the sound:

Listen again and practise saying the words on Rob's shopping list.

b. The sound / ɔː / is a long sound. It is also made at the **back** of the mouth, but the tongue is **higher**. Your lips should look like this:

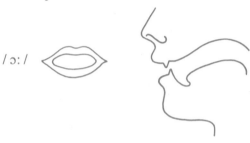

Listen again and practise saying the words on Dawn's shopping list.

c. The sound / əʊ / is a diphthong – it is made with two vowel sounds put together / ə / and / ʊ /. It starts in the **middle** of the mouth and moves slightly **back** and **up**. The first sound is longer than the second. When you make it your lips should look like this:

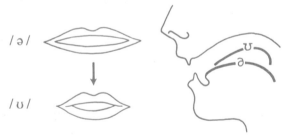

Listen again and practise saying the words on Joan's shopping list.

4 Discuss with a partner which of the items of food on the three lists in 2 are your favourites, which you hate, and which you've never tried.

2 Silent letter 'k'

1 Look at the phonemic transcriptions and write in the words. They all start with silent k.

a. / niː /   k_____

b. / niːl /   k_____

c. / ˈnɪkəz /   k_____

d. / naɪf /   k_____

e. / naɪt /   k_____

f. / nɪt /   k_____

g. / nɒb /   k_____

h. / nɒk /   k_____

i. / nɒt /   k_____

j. / nəʊ /   k_____

k. / ˈnɒlɪdʒ / k_____

l. / ˈnʌkl /   k_____

2 **T.6.2.** Listen and repeat the words. Take care **not** to sound the silent k in each word.

3 Complete the rule:

When k comes before the letter _____ at the beginning of a word it is silent.

● Word focus

Do this exercise after the Vocabulary work on page 52 of the Student's Book.

3 *anti-* and *pro-* words

1 Notice the three medicines on page 52 of your Student's Book which have the prefix *anti-*:

antibiotic   antihistamine   antiseptic cream

What are they all used for? What is the meaning of the prefix *anti-*?

2 *Anti-* is often used as a prefix for words in a **political** or **social** context. Its opposite is *pro-*. The following words can take both *anti-* and *pro-* prefixes. Use a dictionary to check how to pronounce them.

apartheid	nuclear	abortion
American	Soviet	communist
government	feminist	NATO

What is the meaning of the prefix *pro-*?

3 Do you think most people in your country are *pro-* or *anti-* the things above? What about you? Are there any other important issues in your country that many people are very *pro-* or very *anti-*?

4 Use your dictionary to see if you can find any other useful words with the prefix *anti-*.

● Connected speech

4 Linking with *and*

1 **T.6.4.A.** Below are some drinks which are often found together in Britain. Listen to how they are pronounced. What do you notice about the pronunciation of *and*?

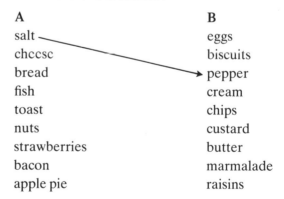

2 Listen and repeat, paying attention to the pronunciation of *and*.

3 Below are some foods which are often found together in Britain. Can you match those in column A with those in column B?

A	B
salt	eggs
cheese	biscuits
bread	pepper
fish	cream
toast	chips
nuts	custard
strawberries	butter
bacon	marmalade
apple pie	raisins

4 **T.6.4.B.** Listen and check your answers.

5 Listen again and repeat the phrases, paying attention to the pronunciation of *and*.

How many of these foods are commonly eaten together in your country? What about the drinks?

● Stress and intonation

Do this exercise after the Controlled Practice on pages 54–5 of the Student's Book.

5 Shifting stress

1 **T.6.5.** In small villages people often know a lot about each other's business! Listen to Alan and Barbara gossiping about the people they know, and mark the main stress in **Barbara's** part like this ■.

a. **A** Had Martin had a few drinks last night?

■

   B He'd had a lot of drinks.

b. **A** Did Caroline buy a new dress yesterday?

   B She bought several dresses.

c. **A** Did the Robinsons lose anything in the burglary?

   B They lost everything in the burglary.

d. **A** I hear Laura's inherited a little money.

   B She's inherited a great deal of money.

e. **A** Jim's been out with quite a few of the girls in the village, hasn't he?

   B Oh, he's been out with all the girls in the village.

f. **A** Have the Smiths spent any of that money they won?

   B Oh, they've spent all the money they won.

g. **A** Does anyone know about you and Pete yet?

   B Oh, everyone knows.

π—0

2 Why do you think these particular words are stressed?

π—0

3 Listen again and repeat **B's** part.

4 Practise reading the dialogues with a partner, paying attention to the stress.

5 Think up some more dialogues like this, using the expressions of quantity on page 54 of the Student's Book.

Do this exercise after the Revision of modal verbs on page 55 of the Student's Book.

6 Giving advice politely

1 **T.6.6.** On the tape you will hear three voices giving advice to Henry, an unfit workaholic, who is having problems with his health.

The voices will give the same advice with **must**, **should** and **ought to**. But one will not sound as polite as the other two. Listen and mark the polite ones like this ✓ and the less polite one like this ✗.

a. ☐ You mustn't smoke so much.
   ☐ You shouldn't smoke so much.
   ☐ You oughtn't to smoke so much.

b. ☐ You must learn to relax more.
   ☐ You should learn to relax more.
   ☐ You ought to learn to relax more.

c. ☐ You must eat more regularly.
   ☐ You should eat more regularly.
   ☐ You ought to eat more regularly.

d. ☐ You mustn't drink so much at lunchtime.

☐ You shouldn't drink so much at lunchtime.

☐ You oughtn't to drink so much at lunchtime.

e. ☐ You must get more exercise.

☐ You should get more exercise.

☐ You ought to get more exercise.

f. ☐ You mustn't work at weekends.

☐ You shouldn't work at weekends.

☐ You oughtn't to work at weekends.

g. ☐ You must take more care of yourself.

☐ You should take more care of yourself.

☐ You ought to take more care of yourself.

🔑—0

2 Which is more important in sounding polite, the modal verb that you choose, or the stress and intonation pattern that you use?

🔑—0

3 Listen again and repeat the sentences with polite intonation, not the less polite ones.

To sound polite, try using the weak forms of **must** and **should**, rather than the strong forms.

	Strong form	Weak form
must	/ mʌst /	/ məst / or / məs /
should	/ ʃʊd /	/ ʃəd /

Don't forget to soften your voice, and make sure your intonation goes up on the last main stress, like this:

You mustn't smoke so much.

You should learn to relax more.

If your intonation is flat and your voice is hard you will sound impolite.

Do this exercise after the Grammar Revision on page 55 of the Student's Book.

7 Intonation with polite requests and offers

1 **T.6.7.A.** All the requests and offers below are things that people might say when one of them is ill. Listen and decide who is speaking in each case – the person who is ill, or the visitor.

a. _____ doctor?

b. _____ aspirin?

c. _____ make _____ tea?

d. _____ open _____ window _____ ?

e. _____ buy _____ magazine

_____ ?

f. _____

prescription _____ ?

g. _____ lift _____

doctor's _____ ?

h. _____ phone the

office _____ ?

i. _____ pop _____ tomorrow?

2 Listen again and fill in the missing words.

🔑—0

3 **T.6.7.B.** Practise the intonation of the requests and the offers. Your voice should start **quite high**, *rise*, and then **go down** on the last important word. Listen and first practise by humming the intonation like this:

de de DE de DE-de?   Shall I call the doctor?

de de DE de de DE-de? Could you get me some aspirin?

4 Listen again and practise saying the sentences, paying attention to the intonation.

5 Work with a partner. Think up a dialogue between a person who is sick and a friend who is visiting. See how many of the sentences above you can include in your dialogue. Can you include any more polite requests and offers?

● Everyday English

Do this exercise before the quiz on page 47 of the Student's Book.

8 International words for talking about nutrition

1 All the words below are used for talking about nutrition. Are they used in your language in the same way? If not, check the meaning in a dictionary.

Vitamin Calorie **Fibre**

Caffeine **Cholesterol**

Carbohydrate Saccharin

Protein Alcohol Mineral

Diet

Calcium Additive Preservative

2 Use your dictionary to find the stress in each word. Then count the number of syllables and put the word into the correct box below.

A ● ●	B ● ● ●
	vitamin

C ● ● ● ●	D ● ● ● ●

3 **T.6.8.** Listen and check your answers.
π—0

4 Listen again and practise saying the words correctly.

9 Saying the time

T.6.9. Many older English people are not familiar with the 'twenty-four hour clock'. Listen to the questions and try to explain what the times are.

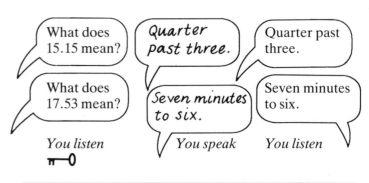

What does 15.15 mean? — *Quarter past three.* — Quarter past three.

What does 17.53 mean? — *Seven minutes to six.* — Seven minutes to six.

You listen π—0 *You speak* *You listen*

Do this exercise after the Vocabulary work on page 50 of the Student's Book.

10 Saying percentages

1 **T.6.10.A.** Listen and practise saying the following percentages.

10%	50%	15%	17%
4%	85%	7.5%	11.3%
99.9%	0.5%	3.45%	19.75%

Where is the stress in the words *per cent*?

2   Below are the statistics for rates of inflation, unemployment and government popularity in the country of Zenia, during the five-year period from 1983 to 1988.

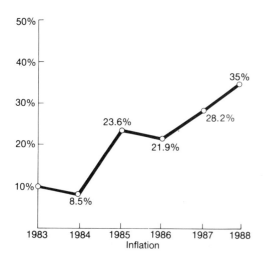

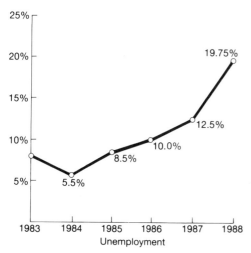

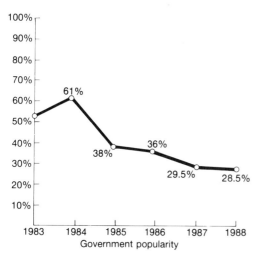

T.6.10.B. Listen and answer the questions on the tape like this:

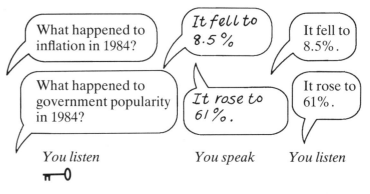

You listen

You speak   *You listen*

UNIT 7

● Sounds and spelling

1 Dark '*l*'

(All Nationalities)

1 **T.7.1.A.** Listen and circle the words you hear.

a. code   cold
b. bored   bald
c. rowed   rolled
d. towed   told
e. word   world

🔑—0

2 When the letter *l* comes at the beginning of a word it is sounded clearly.

To make this **clear *l***, touch the roof of your mouth with your tongue. Use your voice and open your lips to make the sound.

clear / l /

When the sound / l / comes at the middle or at the end of a word it is not so clear.

This kind of *l* is often called **dark *l***. To make this **dark *l*** touch the roof of your mouth with your tongue. Move the back of your tongue up a bit and use your voice and open your lips to make the sound.

dark / l /

3 **T.7.1.B.** Practise saying these words. Try to make a difference between **clear *l*** and **dark *l*.**

late	tale
let	tell
lip	pill
lay	ale
light	tile
law	wall
lied	dial

4 **T.7.1.C.** Listen to these words, and repeat them.

code	cold
bored	bald
rowed	rolled
towed	told
word	world
cord	called
hot	halt
sewed	sold

5 Work with a partner. You say a word and your partner listens and points to the word he or she hears.

42

2 Silent and sounded letter '*l*'

1 The following words all contain a silent letter *l*. Put them into the correct box, according to the preceding vowel sound.

half	yolk	chalk	calm
should	calf	salmon	could
talk	almond	walk	folk
stalk	would	palm	behalf

ɑ:	ɔ:

ʊ	əʊ

æ

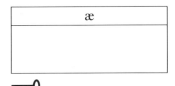

2 **T.7.2.A.** Listen and repeat the words. Take care *not* to sound the letter *l*. Make sure you pronounce the vowel sounds correctly.

3 Complete the rules:

The letters _____ are pronounced / əʊk /.

The letters _____ are pronounced / ɔ: k /.

The letters _____ are pronounced / ʊd /.

The letters _____ are pronounced / ɑ: f /.

The letters _____ are pronounced / ɑ: m / or / æm /.

4 Here are some unusual words which break the rules.

polka	alkaline	salmonella
Dalmation	almost	alfresco
mould	boulder	shoulder

T.7.2.B. Listen and practise saying the words. Take care to sound the letter *l*. Make sure you pronounce the vowel sounds correctly.

5 Do you know any other words with silent *l*?

3 The letters '*ch*'

1 The letters *ch* have two main sound values / tʃ / as in *chip* and / k / as in *chemical*.

Put the following words into the correct column.

chip	bachelor	children	masochist
rich	chance	chemical	choice
Christian	mechanic	champion	character
macho	cholera	technology	research
psychiatric	choir	parched	echo

/ tʃ /	/ k /
chip	*chemical*

2 **T.7.3.A.** Listen and practise saying the words. Make sure you pronounce *ch* correctly.

3 Here are some more words with *ch* in them. Can you pronounce them correctly?

yacht	machine	sachet	chef
chauffeur	champagne	brochure	moustache

4 **T.7.3.B.** Listen and check. How is *ch* pronounced in each case?

5 Listen again and repeat the words.

43

● Word focus

4 Homographs and homonyms

1 A homograph is a word spelt like another, but with a different meaning or pronunciation.

I won't desert you.

They were stuck in the desert.

A homonym is a word spelt and pronounced like another, but with a different meaning.

I'm talking about the present, not the future.

We got her a set of glasses as a leaving present.

T.7.4.A. Listen to the sentences and circle the words you hear.

a. subject   subject

b. minute   minute

c. conduct   conduct

d. minute   minute

e. subject   subject

f. minute   minute

g. conduct   conduct

h. subject   subject

2 How are the underlined words in the following sentences pronounced? Write in the phonemic transcription in each case, selecting from the box below the sentences.

a. They had a big <u>row</u> about money last

night. / _____ /

b. Shall we sit in the back <u>row</u>? / _____ /

c. She had a pink <u>bow</u> in her hair. / _____ /

d. He gave a low <u>bow</u> to the audience.

/ _____ /

e. There was a strong <u>wind</u> blowing.

/ _____ /

f. Can you <u>wind</u> down your window?

/ _____ /

g. <u>Close</u> the door, please. / _____ /

h. You're too <u>close</u> to the microphone.

/ _____ /

i. A large <u>tear</u> rolled down her cheek.

/ _____ /

j. There was a small <u>tear</u> in her dress.

/ _____ /

k. They're broadcasting the concert <u>live</u>.

/ _____ /

l. Where do you <u>live</u>? / _____ /

/ raʊ /	/ rəʊ /	/ kləʊs /	/ kləʊz /
/ baʊ /	/ bəʊ /	/ teə /	/ tɪə /
/ waɪnd /	/ wɪnd /	/ lɪv /	/ laɪv /

3 **T.7.4.B.** Listen and repeat the sentences. Make sure you pronounce the homographs correctly.

44

5 Words ending in -ology, -ologist, and -ological

1 Fill in the grid. (Careful – not all of the forms are regular!)

Subject	Person	Adjective
ecology	ecologist	ecological
	psychologist	
	biologist	
		astrological
	archaeologist	
sociology		
		geological
zoology		
		theological

π—O

2 **T.7.5.** Listen and mark the stress, like this:

• ecology • ecologist • ecological

π—O

3 Listen again and repeat the words. Make sure you put the stress in the correct place.

6 Words ending in -ism

1 Words ending in -ism are often political, religious, or socio-economic beliefs.

Put these words into the correct box according to stress.

feminism	capitalism	optimism
fascism	socialism	Buddhism
Catholicism	communism	cynicism
fatalism	consumerism	pessimism
sexism	realism	chauvinism
materialism	heroism	

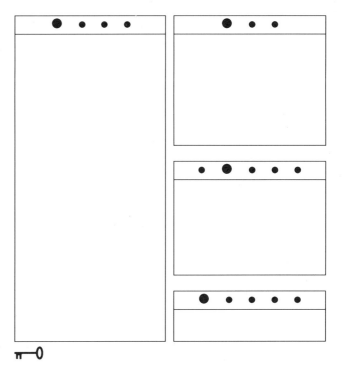

π—O

2 **T.7.6.** Listen and practise saying the words. Make sure you stress them correctly.

3 Complete the following sentences.

a. Feminism is for _feminists_ .

b. Chauvinism is for _____ .

c. Catholicism is for _____ .

d. Buddhism is for _____ .

e. Cynicism is for _____ .

f. Heroism is for _____ and _____ .

π—O

Check in a dictionary to make sure you can pronounce the words above correctly.

● Connected speech

7 Assimilation

1 Look at these words:

Green Party   white meat
White Christmas   Red Brigade

The sound at the end of the first word is changed by the sound at the beginning of the second in each case. If you say the words fast they sound like this:

Gree*m* Party   whi*pe* meat
Whi*ke* Christmas   Re*b* Brigade

This is assimilation. Assimilation happens because the mouth moves into position for the second sound while making the first.

2 **T.7.7.** Listen to the following words. Underline the sound that changes and write what it changes to: / m / / ŋ / / p / / k / / g / or / b /.

whi<u>te</u> gloves /k/   red carpet   green card

red pepper   brown paper   white bread

gold medal   white coffee   brown belt

green goddess   red gold .   Green Movement

white magic   red-brick   white paper
⊓—O

3 Listen again and repeat the words. Say them fast, **with** the assimilation.

4 Complete the rules:

/ t / changes to / _____ / in front of / k / and / g /

and to / _____ / in front of / p /, / m /, and / b /.

/ d / changes to / _____ / in front of / k / and / g /

and to / _____ / in front of / p /, / m /, and / b /.

/ n / changes to / _____ / in front of / k / and / g /

and to / _____ / in front of / p /, / m /, and / b /.

⊓—O

8 Dictation

1 Check that you know what the following words mean, and how they are pronounced.

Big Ben   millennium
ups and downs   New Year's Eve

These words all occur in a passage about the year 2000. What arguments do you think the passage contains?

2 **T.7.8.A.** Listen and check your predictions.

3 **T.7.8.B.** Listen again. This time you will hear the passage broken into short phrases marked by a tone. When you hear the tone, stop the tape and write down the phrases you hear, taking care with punctuation.

4 **T.7.8.C.** Listen again. This time you will hear the passage broken into sentences. Check what you have written, paying attention to spelling and punctuation.
⊓—O

● Stress and intonation

9 Showing degrees of future probability

1 We can show degrees of future probability by the auxiliary verbs we use.

She will come tomorrow.   (certain)

She | might / may / could | come tomorrow.   (possible)

We can also use intonation and stress with *might* and *may* to show if these possibilities are unlikely or not.

2 **T.7.9.A.** Listen to the following sentences.

a. She might come tomorrow.
   (But I don't think she will.)
b. She might come tomorrow.
   (We don't know either way.)
c. He may come later.
   (But I don't think he will.)
d. He may come later.
   (We don't know either way.)

3   Which sentences are unlikely possibilities? Where is the stress in these sentences? What happens to the intonation at the end of these sentences?

What about stress and intonation in the other sentences?

Listen again to find the answers to these questions.

4   Listen again and repeat the sentences with the correct stress and intonation.

5   **T.7.9.B.** Listen to these sentences. Mark the unlikely possibilities *u* .

a. She might come on Wednesday. *u*
b. He may finish it by Christmas.
c. They may arrive soon.
d. I may write to you next week.
e. We may go out this evening.
f. It might rain this afternoon.
g. I might be home late tonight.
h. It may open in January.
i. She may leave on the 20th.
j. He may phone later.
k. They may move out next month.
l. We might go to Greece this summer.

6   Work on your own. Think about any future plans you have and complete the following sentences using *may* or *might*.

a. _____ tonight.
b. _____ tomorrow.
c. _____ next Saturday.
d. _____ next Sunday.
e. _____ next week.
f. _____ next holiday.

Work with a partner. Say one of your sentences. Your partner should decide from your intonation if your future plan is unlikely or not.

● Everyday English

10 Saying large numbers

1   **T.7.10.A.** Listen and repeat these numbers.

> 9   99   999   9,999   99,999   999,999
> 9,999,999

2   **T.7.10.B.** Listen and fill in the numbers.

City	Population
Beijing	9,230,000
Bombay	
Budapest	
Cairo	
London	
Madrid	
Moscow	
Munich	
New York	
Paris	
Rome	
Saõ Paulo	
Sydney	
Tokyo	

(Figures based on the latest census findings available in 1988.)

3   Listen again. This time *you* say the numbers. Make sure you say 'and' in the right places!

4   Work with a partner. In the year 2000 the following cities will be the global top ten in terms of size. Can you put them in order, from 1 to 10, and guess what the population will be in each case?

> Beijing   Calcutta   Mexico City
> Bombay   Jakarta   New York
> Shanghai   Tokyo   Rio de Janeiro
> Saõ Paulo

UNIT 8

● Sounds and spelling

1 The sounds / s / and / ʃ /
Ⓔ Ⓖⓡ Ⓙ

1 **T.8.1.A.** Listen and make sure that you can hear the difference between these pairs of words.

Sue   shoe

sign   shine

suit   shoot

sealed   shield

sore   shore

2 **T.8.1.B.** Work in groups of three. Each person chooses one of the cards below. Listen and cross out the words that you hear on the tape, like this:

~~Sue~~

You will hear each word **twice**.

When you have crossed out a row of words (either **down** or **across**) shout out 'Bingo!', but continue listening to the tape.

A

Sue	rust	short	fist
sewn	fished	shed	shield
shine	shoots	sin	shock
so	seats	shell	shy

B

sore	shown	Sue	rust
sort	shaves	suits	sell
shock	sign	sea	fished
show	sheets	sack	shin

C

sheets	sock	rushed	shoe
she	saves	short	so
shore	shown	sign	sealed
sack	fist	suits	shy

Which card had the first row of crosses?

Which card had the most rows completed?
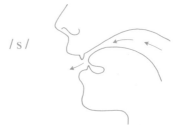

3 Practise the two sounds.

To make the sound / s / your tongue should be raised in the **front** of your mouth like this:

/ s /

You should **not** use your voice.

48

To make the sound / ʃ / your tongue should be further back in your mouth like this:

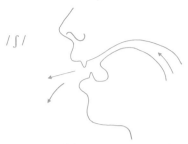

/ ʃ /

You should **not** use your voice.

4   Listen and repeat the pairs of words in 1 above. Make sure that the distinction between the two sounds is clear.

5   **T.8.1.C.**   Listen and repeat these names and phrases.

Shanghai	satin shorts
the suburbs of Sydney	souvenir shop
the Spanish sea shore	disco
the centre of Paris	lots of cash
Sharon Saunders	spent
Sean Stewart	saw
Shirley Smith	said
Simon Sheldrake	shaved
last summer	showed
plastic shoes	selling

6   Work in pairs. Write a mini-story including **as many as possible** of the names and phrases above. Your story should have **exactly** 40 words in it.
⊶—0

7   Practise reading the story aloud, paying attention to the pronunciation of the sounds / s / and / ʃ /.

Read your story to the rest of the class. Who managed to use the most names and phrases?

Do this exercise after the Readings on pages 68–9 of the Student's Book.

2   The pronunciation of 's'
(**All Nationalities**)

1   Below are the phonemic transcriptions of twelve words from the extracts from *The Lotus Eater* on pages 68–9 of the Student's Book. Write in the words.

a.   / sɪˈɡɑː z / _____

b.   / rɒks / _____

c.   / fuː lz / _____

d.   / ɡreɪps / _____

e.   / ˈtʃiː zɪz / _____

f.   / ˈɡɑː mənts / _____

g.   / pəˈdʒɑː məz / _____

h.   / fɪɡz / _____

i.   / ˈmætʃɪz / _____

j.   / ˈfiː tʃəz / _____

k.   / rɪˈflekʃnz / _____

l.   / ˈkɒnfɪdənsɪz / _____
⊶—0

Can you remember what all the words mean?

2   All the words are the plural form, but sometimes this is pronounced / s /, sometimes / z /, and sometimes / ɪz /. Look at the words above again and try to complete the following rules. Then add **three** examples from above.

a.   If the plural *s* comes after a **vowel sound** it is

pronounced _____ . (e.g. _____ /

_____

/ _____)

b.   If the plural *s* comes after a **voiced consonant**

sound (/ b /, / d /, / ɡ /, / v /, / ð /, / m /, / n /, / ŋ /, or

/ l /) then it is pronounced _____ . (e.g.

_____

/ _____

/ _____)

49

c. If the plural *s* comes after a **voiceless consonant**

sound (/ p /, / t /, / k /, / f / or / θ /) then it is

pronounced _____ . (e.g. _____

/ _____ / _____)

d. If the plural *s* comes after an 's-type' sound (/ s /,

/ z /, / ʃ /, / tʃ / or / dʒ /) then it is pronounced

_____ . (e.g. _____ / _____

/ _____)

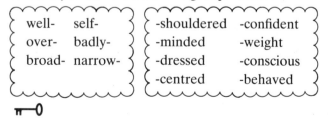

3 How would you pronounce these plural nouns?

illnesses	branches	views	mountains
coffees	uses	pipes	trousers
passions	heads	strengths	brains
existences	delights	remarks	faces

T.8.2.A. Listen and check your answers.

Practise saying the words correctly.

4 **T.8.2.B.** Here are some verbs in the third person singular form, and some nouns with *'s*. Listen and say if the rules above are the same or different.

offers	work's
stands	year's
hurries	heiress's
brushes	lamp's
smiles	moon's
finishes	sun's

Practise saying the words correctly.

5 **T.8.2.C.** Now listen to these words with *s* at the beginning. What is the rule for the pronunciation of *s* + **consonant**?

smile	spine	slave	start
strangers	scraps	small	sleep
spacious	scanty	strength	struck

Listen again and practise saying the words. Be careful not to add a vowel sound before / s /.

Do this exercise after the reading about Cardiff on pages 72–3 of the Student's Book.

3 Silent letter '*t*'

1 Put the words below into the correct column according to whether or not the *t* is silent. There is one word that might go in both columns – which is it?

castle	industry	eastern	Christmas
listen	whistle	often	fasten
faster	gangster	mortgage	soften
youngster	rustle	wrestler	

A *t* is pronounced	**B** *t* is not pronounced

2 **T.8.3.** Listen and check your answers.

3 a. How is *-stle* pronounced at the end of a word?
b. How is *-sten* pronounced at the end of a word?

● Word focus

Do this exercise after the exercise on compound adjectives on page 69 of the Student's Book.

4 Stress in compound adjectives

1 There are twelve compound adjectives in the exercise on page 69 of the Student's Book. Which five can you find from the two groups below?

well-	self-
over-	badly-
broad-	narrow-

-shouldered	-confident
-minded	-weight
-dressed	-conscious
-centred	-behaved

2 You can make at least nine more compound adjectives from the two groups in 1. How many more can you find?

Examples self-confident   broad-minded

3 [T.8.4.A.] Listen and check your answers.

4 Notice the stress in these adjectives. When they are not followed by a noun the **main stress** is on the second word:

● ● ●   ● ●
self-confident   broad-minded

But there is **secondary stress** in the first word:

● ● ● ●   ● ● ●
self-confident   broad-minded

In a dictionary **main** stress is marked like this ', and **secondary** stress is marked like this ,.

,self-'confident   ,broad-'minded

5 Listen and repeat the adjectives on the tape, paying attention to stress.

6 [T.8.4.B.] Listen to the following sentences and mark the **main stress** on the compound adjectives.

a. She's always so well-dressed.

b. They're well-behaved children really.

c. He's so narrow-minded, isn't he?

d. Are you left-handed, Margery?

e. The police are looking for a clean-shaven youth who was spotted at the scene of the crime.

f. Sharon's got a really good-looking boyfriend.

g. Don't be so self-centred!

h. It's difficult working for a bad-tempered boss.

i. I'm not going to marry an overweight businessman!

Is the stress always on the second word? Can you find the rule?

7 Work with a partner. Each choose a person that you both know very well and decide which of these adjectives could be used to describe that person. Write a short description and read it out to your partner. Does your partner know who it is?

● **Connected speech**

Do this exercise after the Revision exercise with *get* on page 75 of the Student's Book.

5 Understanding fast speech

1 [T.8.5.] Write the number of words you hear in each sentence in the box on the left (*I'm* = **two** words).

a. [6] _can I get you past you_ , please?

b. [ ] _get me_   _a pair of_ scissors, _will you_ ?

c. [ ] _So what_ time _did you get_ _back form ._ party?

d. [ ] Sorry, _I just get couldn't get_ _away from I_ the office.

e. [ ] Unfortunately _we couldn't_ _get inter to the_ stadium.

f. [ ] _get in touch with me as_ soon _as you get to the_ airport, _won't you_ ?

g. [ ] _I shouldn't_ think _'ll get in before_ midnight.

h. [ ] _I'll get you_ something _to drink_, _shall I_ ?

2 Listen again and fill in the missing words.

3 Listen again and repeat the sentences, paying attention to any weak forms.

4 Rewrite the sentences using these verbs:

pass	leave	enter
reach	fetch	contact
arrive home	return	fetch

● Stress and intonation

Do this exercise after the exercise on expressing negative qualities on page 70 of the Student's Book.

6 Criticizing tactfully

1 Match the adjectives in column **A** with their opposites in column **B**.

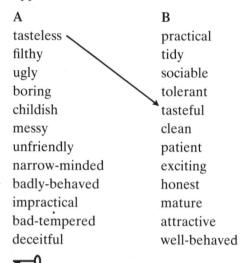

A	B
tasteless	practical
filthy	tidy
ugly	sociable
boring	tolerant
childish	tasteful
messy	clean
unfriendly	patient
narrow-minded	exciting
badly-behaved	honest
impractical	mature
bad-tempered	attractive
deceitful	well-behaved

2 Two people are discussing a family they know. They are making a lot of criticisms. Use some of the adjectives above to complete these dialogues.

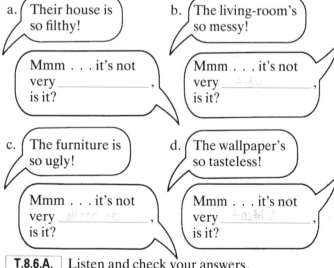

a. Their house is so filthy!

Mmm . . . it's not very _____, is it?

b. The living-room's so messy!

Mmm . . . it's not very _tidy_, is it?

c. The furniture is so ugly!

Mmm . . . it's not very _attractive_, is it?

d. The wallpaper's so tasteless!

Mmm . . . it's not very _tasteful_, is it?

3 **T.8.6.A.** Listen and check your answers.

Who is more tactful in their criticism, the first speaker or the second? In what way?

4 Notice the stress and intonation in each case:

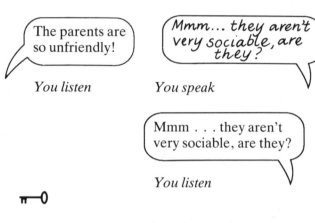

A Their house is so filthy!

B Mmm . . . it's not very clean, is it?

5 Listen again and repeat the dialogues, paying attention to stress and intonation.

6 **T.8.6.B.** Listen to **A** making some more criticisms and take **B**'s part, paying attention to stress and intonation. Use the pairs of adjectives above like this:

The parents are so unfriendly!

You listen

Mmm... they aren't very sociable, are they?

You speak

Mmm . . . they aren't very sociable, are they?

You listen

"MMM, THEY AREN'T VERY WELL BEHAVED, ARE THEY?"

Do this exercise after the exercise on sentence building on page 74 of the Student's Book.

7 Corrective stress

1   Read this article from a local newspaper.

> A TALL, DARK-HAIRED man in his mid-thirties, wearing an expensive-looking white suit and carrying a gun, last night robbed Springfield village post office and got away with £10,000 in cash.

2   **T.8.7.A.** Now listen to this dialogue between a local newspaper reporter (**A**) and a witness (**B**). Write in all the mistakes that **A** makes as he is speaking. Write only one word like this:

a. *short*   e. _____

b. _____   f. _____

c. _____   g. _____

d. _____

3   Listen again and write in the word that **B** most stresses each time.

a. *tall*   e. _____

b. _____   f. _____

c. _____   g. _____

d. _____

Why does **B** stress this word in each case, do you think?

π—0

4   Listen again and repeat **B**'s part, paying attention to stress.

5   Now read this article from the same paper, and try to memorize the information in it.

MRS LILY PARKINSON, a seventy-five-year-old Springfield woman, who was carrying just a shopping bag and a purse containing £1.50, was attacked at a bus stop yesterday in broad daylight by three youths wearing leather jackets and carrying knives.

6   **T.8.7.B.** Listen to the newspaper reporter speaking and take **B**'s part, like this:

> . . . so the woman was sixty-five years old . . .?

You listen

> No, she was seventy-five years old.

You speak

> No, she was seventy-five years old.

You listen

π—0

Do this exercise after the exercise on modifiers on page 75 of the Student's Book.

8 Showing strong and mixed feelings

1 **T.8.8.A.** Listen to these short dialogues. In each dialogue you will hear two adjectives. Write in the adjectives that you hear.

a. _____ / _____

b. _____ / _____

c. _____ / _____

d. _____ / _____

2 Which person showed the strongest feelings in each case? How do we know? How does the other person show that they have mixed feelings?
π—0

3 **T.8.8.B.** Notice the intonation in each case:

de DE-de-de-de de-DE-de, de DE?

I'm absolutely exhausted, aren't you?

DE . . . de DE DE.

Well . . . I'm quite tired.

de DE de DE de DE-de-de-de de-DE-de,

de-de DE?

I thought the meal was absolutely delicious, didn't you?

DE . . . de de DE DE-de.

Well . . . it was quite tasty.

4 Listen and repeat the four dialogues, paying attention to intonation.

5 Work with a partner. Make two or three similar dialogues using some of the prompts below.

a. (THE SEA) freezing/cold
b. (THE EXHIBITION) fascinating/interesting
c. (THE PLAY) hilarious/funny
d. (THE BOOK) marvellous/good
e. (THESE CARTOONS) brilliant/clever

● Everyday English

Do this exercise after the Vocabulary exercise on page 72 of the Student's Book.

9 Words for describing shapes

1 Write these nouns next to the correct shape below. Can you make the adjectives from these nouns, as in the example?

cube	curve	cylinder	triangle
sphere	hexagon	rectangle	semi-circle
square	oval	circle	octagon

a. *triangle*
triangular

g. _____

b. _____

h. _____

c. _____

i. _____

d. _____

j. _____

e. _____

k. _____

f. _____

l. _____

2 **T.8.9.A.** Listen and check your answers. As you listen, mark the stress on the words.
π—0

3 Listen and practise saying the words with the correct stress.

4 Notice the change in stress:

triangle triangular

Which other pairs of words have a similar change of stress? Practise saying these pairs of words with the stress in the correct place.

5 **T.8.9.B.** Take a piece of paper and draw what you hear on the tape.

Compare your drawing with the one in the answer key.
π—0

UNIT 9

● Sounds and spelling

1 The sounds / b / and / v /
Ⓔ Ⓙ

1 | T.9.1.A. | Can you hear the difference between the sounds / b / and / v /? Listen to these pairs of words and number them according to the order that you hear them, 1 or 2.

a. ☐ ban   ☐ van
b. ☐ best   ☐ vest
c. ☐ bars   ☐ vase
d. ☐ boats   ☐ votes
e. ☐ bet   ☐ vet
f. ☐ berry   ☐ very
g. ☐ fibre   ☐ fiver
h. ☐ dub   ☐ dove

⛏—0

2   Practise making the two sounds. To start the sound / b /, **both** lips should touch each other.

a.   b.

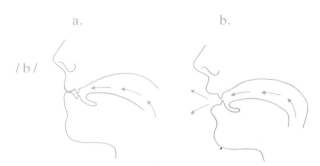

/ b /

You should use your voice to make the sound.

To make the sound / v /, your **top** teeth should touch your **bottom** lip like this:

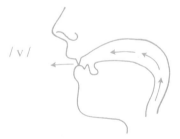

/ v /

Again, you should use your voice.

3   Listen again and practise saying the two words. Make sure that the difference between them is clear.

4   Write six of the words in 1 above on a piece of paper. Dictate them to your partner and then compare your lists of words. Are they the same?

5 **T.9.1.B.** Below are some headlines from a sensational Sunday newspaper. Listen and then practise saying them. Pay attention to the pronunciation of / b / and / v /.

British Van Driver Banned from Costa Brava Bar

Bomb Victim Vivienne Gives Birth to Baby Boy

Brighton Vicar Leaves 'Boring' Wife for Blonde Barmaid

Brave Bob Saves Baby Vicki from Blazing Bedroom

Violent Bolivian Lover Obsessed by Vow of Revenge

2 Silent letter 'b'

1. Cross out the silent *b*s in the words below.

lamb	climb	bombardment	thumb
combination	numb	bomb	dumb
comb	number	crumb	debt
limb	doubt	crumble	plumber
limbo	subtle	subtitle	lumber

2 **T.9.2.A.** Listen and practise saying the words with silent letter *b*.

3 **T.9.2.B.** Listen and practise saying the other words.

4 Complete the rule:

When the letters *mb* or *bt* come at the end of a word.

b is _____. Some other words, like

_____ and _____, for

example, also contain silent ____.

Do this exercise at the end of Unit 9 of the Student's book.

3 The letters 'ea'

1 All the words below come from Unit 9 and have vowel sounds spelt with *ea*. Can you remember what they all mean?

health	heard	appeared
feature	leave	yeah
earn	rehearsing	ideal
wears	leather	increases
theatre	break	colleagues
pleased	teacher	death

2 Put the words into the correct box, according to the pronunciation of *ea*.

A / e /	B / ɪə /
health	

C / iː /	D / ɜː /

E / eɪ /	F / eə /

3 **T.9.3.** Listen and check your answers.

4 Which is the most common pronunciation of *ea*? Can you think of any more words spelt with *ea* to add to each box?

5 The pairs of words below have the same spelling but *ea* is pronounced differently. What does each word mean?

/ iː / / e /   / ɪə / / eə /   / iː / / e /
lead lead   tear tear   read read

Use a dictionary to help you if you are not sure.

6 Test your partner. Make a list of any ten of the words in this exercise and see how many your partner can pronounce correctly. Try to choose words that you think your partner might confuse!

● Word focus

Do this exercise at the beginning of Unit 9.

4 More complex family relationships

1 Work in pairs. Use a dictionary to help you to explain the difference between these relations.

a. my nephew and my niece
b. my uncle and my aunt
c. my cousin and my second cousin
d. my aunt and my great-aunt
e. my grandson and my great-grandson
f. my stepbrother, my half-brother and my brother-in-law
g. my ex-wife and my wife-to-be

2 **T.9.4.A.** Listen and mark the **main** stress in these words.

a. granddaughter   f. great-nephew
b. great-grandmother g. second cousin
c. ex-husband   h. mother-in-law
d. stepmother   i. ex-boyfriend
e. half-sister   j. son-in-law
⊓—0

3 Listen again and practise saying the words with the correct stress.

4 **T.9.4.B.** Listen to these descriptions and write down which relation is being described.

a. _____   e. _____
b. _____   f. _____
c. _____   g. _____
d. _____   h. _____
⊓—0

Do this exercise after the exercise on words commonly confused on page 82 of the Student's Book.

5 Words commonly confused because of their pronunciation

1 Do you know the meaning of the words below? Use a dictionary to check any that you are not sure of.

a. rise / raɪz /
   raise / reɪz /

b. breathe / briː ð /
   breath / breθ /

c. use / juː z /
   use / juː s /

d. bathe / beɪð /
   bath / bɑː θ /

2 Use the phonemic transcription to work out the difference in pronunciation.

3 **T.9.5.A.** Listen and check your answers and then practise saying the words correctly.

4 Decide which word is correct in each of the sentences below. Cross out the incorrect words.

a. If you agree, *rise/raise* your hand.
b. Why are you so out of *breathe/breath*?
c. What's the *use* / juː z / / *use* / juː s / of arguing?
d. She watched the sun *rise* / *raise* over the mountain top.
e. *Breathe* / *breath* deeply and relax.
f. I'm going to *bathe* / *bath* the baby.
g. Can I *use* / juː s / / *use* / juː z / your pen?
h. You must *bathe* / *bath* that cut in salt water.

5 **T.9.5.B.** Listen and check your answers. Practise reading the sentences making sure that you pronounce the words correctly.
⊓—0

● Connected speech

Do this exercise after looking at the idiomatic expressions on page 80 of the Student's Book.

6 Word linking

1 When we speak quickly, words often link together:

If the second word starts with a vowel, and the first word ends with a vowel sound the sounds / w / and / j / can link the two words together:

/ w /   / j /
no‿idea   I‿agree   (See Unit 2.1.)

If the second word begins with a vowel, the consonant at the end of the first word can link on to it:

Out‿of‿Africa
sooner‿or later   (See Unit 2.6 and Unit 3.6.)

If the second word begins with a consonant, and the first word ends with a consonant or two, the final consonant of the first word can disappear:

Min̸d the step
Gin an̸d Tonic   (See Unit 5.6 and Unit 6.4.)

If the second word begins with a consonant, the consonant at the end of the first word can change so that it is more similar to the one that follows:
/m/   /k/
Gree̸n Party   Whi̸te coffee   (See Unit 7.7.)

2 Work in pairs. Look at the expressions below and discuss how they might be linked together if they were said quickly.

a. We're as different as chalk and cheese.

b. Patrick and Jenny get on like a house on fire.

c. It was love at first sight.

d. She really gets on my nerves.

e. They're head over heels in love.

f. We're not on speaking terms any more.

g. They don't see eye to eye on anything.

3 **T.9.6.** Listen and check your answers.
π—0

4 Listen again and practise saying the expressions quickly, linking the words together where possible.

Do this exercise after the Controlled Practice on page 82 of the Student's Book.

7 Weak forms with modals of deduction

1 **T.9.7.A.** Listen and fill in the missing words in these dialogues.

a. _____ snowing _____ ?

No, _____ – it's _____ the _____ year _____ .

b. _____ snack bar _____ _____ good?

_____ – everyone in _____ _____ lunch.

c. _____ home _____ ?

No, _____ _____ – his _____ _____ here .

d. _____ Simon _____ ?

I _____ _____ – he seemed _____ _____ me.

2 What do you notice about the pronunciation of the auxiliaries *be* and *have* with the modal verbs?
π—0

Listen again and repeat, paying attention to the weak forms of *have* and *be*.

3 **T.9.7.B.** Now listen and respond using the information below like this:

Example a. Everything's so quiet.

> Are the children sleeping?

You listen

> They must be sleeping — everything's so quiet.

You speak

> They must be sleeping — everything's so quiet.

You listen

b. She's gone to work.
c. She looks a lot slimmer.
d. All the lights are off.
e. She's got a new boyfriend.
f. He's just bought a new car.
g. They're always together.
h. I saw them in the garden this morning.
i. She's been on the phone for hours.
j. He sounds so British.

—o

---

8 Reading aloud

1 **T.9.8.A.** Listen to the following reading passage. Read the text silently as you listen.

I was fifteen. He was nineteen and already doing well. He was a tailor like his father and worked with him. One day my grandmother came and called me. She took me to one side and said,

'Zeina, you're going to marry Sobhi.'

'But, Setti, how do I marry him?' I asked.

He was my cousin: the son of my dead mother's sister, but I knew nothing of marriage.

'You'll be his wife and he'll be your husband and you'll serve him and do what he tells you.'

I started to cry.

'Will I have to leave you, Setti?'

The old woman took me in her arms:

'No, no, you'll have your own room in the house and I'll always be with you. You're a big girl now. You can cook and clean and look after a man and he's your cousin, child, he's not a stranger.'

Well . . . I went out to the other girls in the yard but my heart was full of my new importance. I didn't say anything but in a few hours everyone knew anyway and Sobhi stopped coming to our part of the house. From the time Setti told me, I only saw him again on the wedding night.

2 **T.9.8.B.** You will now hear the same passage broken up into short phrases. Listen and repeat each phrase, paying attention to word-linking and to intonation.

3 **T.9.8.C.** You will now hear the same passage broken up into longer sentences. Listen and repeat each sentence, paying attention to intonation and phrasing.

4 Now read the whole passage through aloud, paying attention to phrasing and to pace.

● Stress and intonation

Do this exercise after Language Review on pages 80–1 of the Student's Book.

9 Intonation in *Wh-* questions

1 **T.9.9.A.** Most often the intonation of questions beginning with *Wh-* words goes **down** at the end.

> Jim and Sandra have announced their engagement.

> When did they announce it?

2 **T.9.9.B.** But to show surprise or disbelief in a *Wh-* question, the intonation goes **up**:

> Ben suggested that we should get married.

> What did he suggest?

3 **T.9.9.C.** First practise by humming like this:

DE de de de-DE de?   When did they announce it?

DE de de de-DE?   What did he suggest?

4 **T.9.9.D.** Listen and mark the box ↘ if the intonation goes down, and ↗ if the intonation goes up.

a. **A** Chris apologized for not inviting me the other night.

   B Why did she apologize?

b. **A** Jenny asked Jason to go to the office party with her.

   B Who did she ask?

c. **A** Rob's offered to lend me £2,000.

   B What's he offered to do?

d. **A** Colin denied that he was going out with Liz.

   B Why did he deny it?

e. **A** Rita explained her behaviour the other night.

   B How did she explain it?

f. **A** Judy was complaining that nobody ever talks to her.

   B Why was she complaining?

π—0

5 Look back at the questions where the intonation goes up and try to imagine a reason why the person is surprised in the situation.
π—0

6 Listen again and repeat **B**'s part, paying attention to your intonation.

7 Work in pairs.

Student A Fill in the grid below with the name of a person, a place, and a thing that is important to you.

Person	
Place	
Thing	

Student B Look at **A**'s grid, and ask some *Wh-* questions to get more information from **A** about his/her person, place and thing.

Example
Who is Sue?
Where did you meet her?
Why is Paris so important to you?
What did you do there?
Where did you get your emerald ring?
How much is it worth?

10 Stress in multi-word verbs

1 The most common type of multi-word verbs follow the pattern below.

She took off her hat. (+ noun object)
She took her hat off. (+ noun object)
She took it off. (+ pronoun object)

T.9.10.A. Listen to these sentences and mark the stress patterns like this ■.

a. She took off her hat.

b. She took her hat off.

c. She took it off.
π—0

2 **T.9.10.B.** Listen and respond, changing the noun object into a pronoun object each time, like this. (Make sure you stress the sentences correctly.)

> They're going to pull down the old school.

> The old school?

> Yes, they're going to pull it down.

You listen   *You listen*   *You speak*
π—0

11 Ranks and titles

1 Hidden in the square below are the names of 34 ranks and titles in different areas of public life. You have ten minutes to find as many as you can and put them into the correct column opposite.

G	E	N	E	R	A	L	S	E	C	R	E	T	A	R	Y
Q	U	E	E	N	M	E	M	P	E	R	O	R	C	D	V
A	S	C	L	B	B	C	H	A	I	R	M	A	N	D	I
P	E	A	O	R	A	R	C	H	B	I	S	H	O	P	C
R	R	R	R	A	S	M	O	P	R	I	N	C	E	O	A
I	G	D	D	B	S	O	L	S	H	E	I	K	H	P	R
M	E	I	L	B	A	C	O	U	N	T	E	S	S	E	G
E	A	N	A	I	D	P	N	D	C	O	N	S	U	L	U
M	N	A	D	J	O	N	E	U	E	M	P	R	E	S	S
I	T	L	Y	R	R	Q	L	K	L	K	S	H	A	H	I
N	T	V	I	C	E	P	R	E	S	I	D	E	N	T	J
I	P	R	I	N	C	E	S	S	C	O	U	N	T	U	V
S	S	C	H	A	N	C	E	L	L	O	R	W	X	Y
T	A	D	E	B	D	U	C	H	E	S	S	K	I	N	G
E	A	D	M	I	R	A	L	C	A	P	T	A	I	N	Z
R	L	L	I	E	U	T	E	N	A	N	T	F	K	R	Z

A Political/Diplomatic	B Royal/Aristocratic
Prime Minister	

C Religious	D Military/Naval

2 **T.9.11.** Listen and check your answers. How many did you find?
π—0

3 Listen again and practise saying the words correctly.

4 Which of these titles still exist in your country today? Which used to exist in the past? Which other countries are these ranks often associated with?

UNIT 10

● Sounds and spelling

1 Silent letter 'p'

1 Fill in the crossword. All the words have a silent *p*.

```
1  P | | | | | | | | |
2  P | | | | | | | |
3  P | | | | |
4  P | | | | |
5  P | | | | |
6  P | | | | | | | |
7  | | P | | | | | |
8  | | | | P | |
9  P | | | | |
10 P | | | | |
```

Clues
1. Person who studies the human mind.
2. Flying dinosaur.
3. Serious illness which affects the lungs, making it difficult to breathe.
4. Name which a writer uses instead of his real name. Eric Arthur Blair's . . . was George Orwell.
5. A . . . drill is a drill powered by compressed air.
6. A doctor who treats people suffering from mental illnesses is called a . . . .
7. A piece of furniture which has one or two doors and usually has shelves inside.
8. You get a . . . when you buy something. It's a piece of paper which gives the details of your purchase – the price paid, the date, etc.
9. . . . powers are mental powers – such as mind-reading – which science cannot explain.
10. One of 150 songs, poems or prayers from a book of the Bible.

⚲—0

2 **T.10.1.** Now listen and repeat. Take care not to sound the *p* in each word.

3 Complete the rule:

The initial letter *p* is silent in words that begin with

_____ , _____ , and _____ . Some other words like

_____ and _____ , for example, also

contain silent *p*.

⚲—0

2 The letters 'gh'

1   Put the following words into the correct columns according to the pronunciation of *gh*.

rough	ghost	laughter
ghastly	plough	cough
through	slaughter	tough
drought	gherkin	ghoulish

/ f /	silent *gh*
rough	*plough*

/ g /
ghost

2   Use a dictionary to check the meaning of any words which are new to you.

3   **T.10.2.A.** Listen and practise saying the words.

4   Now put the words in sentences like this:

They lived *through* the *drought*.
What's that *ghoulish laughter*?
These *gherkins* are *tough*!

5   **T.10.2.B.** Listen and practise reading these sentences, and your sentences, aloud.

6   Complete the rule:

When the letters *gh* come at the beginning of a word

they are always pronounced   .

3 The letter 'u'

1   The letter *u* can be pronounced in different ways. Put the following words into the correct columns.

pudding	amused	bush	utensil
lucky	rude	conclusion	pub
flute	unite	puzzle	bullet

/ ʌ /	/ ʊ /
puzzle	*pudding*

/ u: /	/ ju: /
rude	*unite*

2   **T.10.3.A.** Listen and practise saying the words. Make sure you pronounce the *u* sounds correctly.

3   Write some sentences with *u* sounds in them.

Rubik's cube's an amusing puzzle.
Who's used my new blue toothbrush?
He used to be a tutor at London University.

4   **T.10.3.B.** Listen and practise reading these sentences, and your own, aloud.

5   Transcribe the following words. They all contain *gu* or *qu*.

a. / tʃek / _ _ _ *qu_*   g. / ˌgærən'ti: /

b. / veɪg / _ _ *gu_*   *gu_ _ _ _ _ _*

c. / gɑ: d / *gu_ _ _*   h. / kju: / *qu_ _ _*

d. / 'kwaɪət / *qu_ _ _*   i. / 'bæŋkwɪt /

e. / kwaɪt / *qu_ _ _*   _ _ _ *qu_ _*

f. / gest / *gu_ _ _*   j. / bʊ'keɪ / _ _ _ *qu_ _*

6   **T.10.3.C.** Listen and repeat the words. Make sure you pronounce *gu* and *qu* correctly each time.

● Word focus

4 Opposites with *un-* and *dis-*

1 Opposites from the following adjectives can be formed using *un-* or *dis-*, and sometimes both.

Complete the chart. One word changes meaning with *un-* and *dis-*. Which is it?

	un-	*dis-*
tidy	untidy	———
adventurous		
satisfied		
comfortable		
reliable		
sociable		
honest		
agreeable		
interested		
loyal		
reasonable		
acceptable		

2 **T.10.4.** Listen and check your answers.

3 Listen again. This time write the words in the correct column according to word stress.

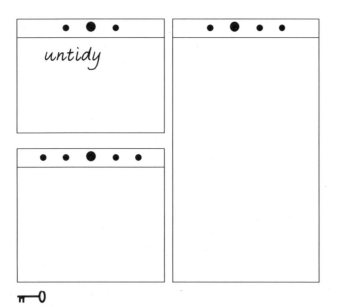

4

Listen again and practise saying the words. Make sure you put the stress in the correct place – the second or third syllable – and that the prefixes *dis-* and *un-* are unstressed.

5 Use a dictionary to check the meaning of any new words and write some example sentences like these:

He was an unadventurous, stay-at-home type.
This sofa's most uncomfortable. It's so hard!

● Connected speech

5 Animal and other idioms

1 Here are some well-known English animal idioms in phonemic script. Can you transcribe them?

a. / ʃiː z əzˈblaɪnd əz ə bæt /

_____

b. / hiː z əzˈstʌbən əz əˈmjuː l /

_____

c. / ʃiː z əzˈstrɒŋ əz ənˈɒks /

_____

d. / hiː z əzˈpraʊd əz ə ˈpiː kɒk /

_____

e. / hiː ˈdrɪŋks laɪk əˈfɪʃ /

_____

f. / ʃiː ˈiːts laɪk əˈpɪg /

_____

64

2　[T.10.5.]　Listen and repeat. Pay attention to the weak forms and the rhythm of the sentences.

3　Fill in the gaps in these idioms, using the words in the box below.

   a.　She smokes like *a chimney*   .

   b.　He swears like _____ .

   c.　He's as mad as _____ .

   d.　She's as fit as _____ .

   e.　The children were as good as _____ .

   f.　She's as ugly as _____ .

   g.　It's as heavy as _____ .

   h.　I slept like _____ .

a trooper	lead	a hatter	a fiddle
sin	gold	a log	a chimney

♬—0

4　Practise saying these idioms paying attention to the weak forms and the rhythm as before.

6　*used to*, *be/get used to*, and *usually*

1　Complete these foreign visitors' statements about living in Britain, using either *used to*, *usually*, or a form of *be used to* or *get used to*.

'I _____ drink tea. It's better than the coffee here.'

'I can't _____ the British weather. It's so changeable.'

'I _____ driving on the right, not the left.'

'I _____ think double-decker buses were very strange before I came to London.'

2　[T.10.6.A.]　Listen and check your answers.
♬—0

3　Listen again and repeat the sentences. Make sure you pronounce *used to* / ˈjuː stə / and *usually* / ˈjuː ʒəlɪ / correctly.

4　Complete the answers to these questions. Use either *used to* or a form of *be/get used to*. Remember that *be/get used to* needs an object. (*I'm used to it.*)

   a.　Does your mother wash and dress you nowadays?

     No, but _____ .

   b.　Why don't English people hate warm beer?

     Because _____ .

   c.　Are there any wolves living wild in Britain these days?

     No, but _____ .

   d.　Do you find British English more difficult to follow than American English?

     Yes, but I'm slowly _____ .

   e.　Do you think the Prime Minister minds all the political cartoons of her?

     No, I expect _____ .

   f.　How can Italians drink such strong coffee?

     They _____ .

   g.　Do you suck your thumb these days?

     No, but _____ .

   h.　Did you find the traditional English breakfast strange at first?

     Yes, but I soon _____ .

5　[T.10.6.B.]　Listen and check your answers.
♬—0

6　Listen again. This time cover the book and say the answers.

Does your mother wash and dress you nowadays? | *No, but she used to.* | No, but she used to.

You listen　　*You speak*　　*You listen*
♬—0

7　[T.10.6.C.]　Listen and complete the questions.

   a.　When do you usually _____ ?

   b.　Where do you usually _____ ?

   c.　What do you usually _____ ?

d. Who do you usually _____ ?

e. What do you usually _____ ?

f. When do you usually _____ ?

g. What do you usually _____ ?

h. Where do you usually _____ ?

🔑—O

8   Listen again. This time answer the questions. Be truthful.

---

7   Unpronounced plosives

1   The sounds / d /, / t /. / b /, / p /, / g / and / k / are called plosive sounds. To make them we release air suddenly in an 'explosion'. Often when two of these sounds occur together the first plosive is not pronounced.

   T.10.7.A. Listen to the following phrases. Can you hear any difference between the phrases on the left and the phrases on the right?

red eye	red dye
bright eyes	bright ties
her bread	herb bread
top layer	top player
big eight	big gate
black ape	black cape

   🔑—O

2   Listen again and practise saying the phrases correctly.

3   **T.10.7.B.** Listen and cross out the unpronounced plosive sounds in the following sentences.

   a. She was wearing a deep purple evening dress.
   b. They had dinner at nine o'clock.
   c. We've got a flat tyre, I'm afraid.
   d. She gave him a quick kiss.
   e. You're a big girl now, dear.
   f. He didn't do the washing-up.
   g. We had a really good time at Antonia's.
   h. What are my job prospects after the course?
   i. Mmm! I love ripe bananas!
   j. Give that ball a big kick!
   k. They've got a lovely back garden.

   🔑—O

4   Listen again and practise saying the sentences correctly.

● Stress and intonation

8   Echo questions

1   Write in the opposites of the following adjectives that describe a person's character or appearance.

   a. taciturn   *talkative*

   b. brave   _____

   c. proud   _____

   d. plain   _____

   e. well brought-up   _____

   f. tight-fisted   _____

   g. big-headed   _____

   h. lazy   _____

   i. naive   _____

humble	spoilt	talkative
modest	hard-working	generous
sophisticated	cowardly	attractive

   🔑—O

2   Look at this dialogue:

   A Arthur's so taciturn.
   B Arthur's taciturn? I thought he was rather talkative myself.

   The normal word order for questions is: 'Is Arthur taciturn?' But here **B** is using statement word order – echoing A's words – to show surprise and to question A's opinion. To make a statement into an echo question the intonation changes.

   Statement   Arthur's taciturn.

   Echo question Arthur's taciturn?

   T.10.8.A. Listen to the following phrases. Put in a full-stop (.) after each statement, and a question mark (?) after each echo question.

   a. Arthur's taciturn
   b. Jane's brave
   c. Julian's proud
   d. Andrea's plain
   e. Amanda's well brought-up
   f. Paul's tight-fisted
   g. Sally's big-headed
   h. Peter's lazy
   i. Mary's naive

   🔑—O

3 Listen again. This time repeat the statements and echo questions. Take care to use the correct intonation.

4 **T.10.8.B.** Now listen and respond.

Arthur's so taciturn!

You listen

Arthur's taciturn?
I thought he was
rather talkative
myself.

You speak

Arthur's taciturn?
I thought he was
rather talkative myself.

You listen

9 *would* or *had*

1 **T.10.9.** Cover the sentences below and listen to them on the tape. Say whether the contraction *'d* is *would* or *had* in each case. You should listen to each sentence **once** only and should **not** stop the tape.

2 Listen again and write the missing words into the sentences.

a. I _____ tea with lemon _____ .

b. _____ school holidays _____ .

c. You _____ a taxi, darling.

d. You _____ the airport _____ .

e. _____
_____ the opera.

f. _____
_____ expensive presents.

g. _____
straight to bed _____ .

h. She _____ another job.

i. I _____ married to a miser.

j. He _____ desert island _____ .

3 Listen again and practise saying the sentences. Make sure you stress them correctly.

● Everyday English

10 Different currencies

1 Write the currency next to the nationality.

Australian *dollars*   Greek _____

Austrian _____   Italian _____

Danish _____   Japanese _____

Dutch _____   Portuguese _____

French _____   Spanish _____

German _____   Yugoslav _____

2 **T.10.10.** Listen to the exchange rates and fill in the table.

£1 buys:

_____	dinars	_____	kroner
_____	dollars	_____	lire
_____	drachmas	_____	marks
_____	escudos	_____	pesetas
_____	francs	_____	schillings
_____	guilders	_____	yen

3 Using the conversion table above, work out how much I paid to get the following.

a. 3,224 drachmas   d. 30,525 pesetas
b. 7,152 yen   e. 96,000 dinars
c. 34,500 lire   f. 18,975 escudos

4 Can you match up the currency and the country?

zloty   USSR
rouble   Hungary
forint   Israel
shekel   Poland

UNIT 11

● Sounds and spelling

1 The sounds /dʒ/ and /tʃ/
ⓓ ⓗ

1 **T.11.1.A.** Listen and circle the words you hear.

   a. joking   choking
   b. badge   batch
   c. jeers   cheers
   d. surging   searching
   e. gin   chin
   🔑━O

2 Practise making the sounds.

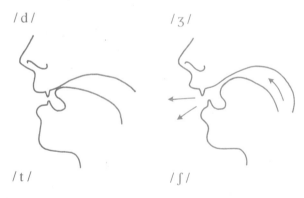

/d/   /ʒ/

/t/   /ʃ/

/dʒ/ is a combination of /d/ and /ʒ/.
It is voiced.

/tʃ/ is a combination of /t/ and /ʃ/.
It is voiceless.

T.11.1.B. Listen and repeat these words:

/dʒ/	/tʃ/
joke	choke
badge	batch
jeer	cheer
surge	search
gin	chin
jeep	cheap

3 Look at the reading text about Jack Higgins on page 93 of the Student's Book. It contains twenty-one words, excluding proper names and nationalities, with either the sound /dʒ/ or the sound /tʃ/. Find them and put them into the correct column below.

/dʒ/	/tʃ/
original	teacher

4 **T.11.1.C.** Listen and check your answers.
🔑━O

5 Listen again and practise saying the words.

2 Different pronunciations of 's'

1 The letter *s* can be pronounced in four different ways. Put the following words into the correct columns.

insult	please	leisure	surely
usually	ensure	pleasure	goose
result	sure	sugar	lose
increase	vase	dose	treasure
choose	insurance	chase	casual

/ s /	/ z /
insult	*please*

/ ʃ /	/ ʒ /
surely	*Leisure*

π—0

2 **T.11.2.A.** Listen and practise saying the words. Make sure you pronounce the letter *s* correctly each time.

3 Look at the following groups of words and circle the odd one out in each group according to the pronunciation of *s*.

a. percussion   c. assume
   permission   assure
   permissive   issue
   concussion   pressure

b. mansion   d. dishonest
   pension   disheartened
   expansion   dishevelled
   conclusion   dishonourable

π—0

4 **T.11.2.B.** Listen and practise saying the groups of words. Make sure you pronounce them all correctly.

5 Make short sentences. Use three of the *s* words you've practised each time, like this:

I *assume* you've got *permission* to dig for *treasure*.
It's a wild *goose chase*, I *assure* you!
Are you *sure* he said *increase* the *dose*?
Please ensure you don't *lose* this card.
He isn't *usually casual* or *dishevelled*.

6 **T.11.2.C.** Listen and read these sentences, and yours, aloud.

3 The letters '*ph*'

1 The letters *ph* are usually pronounced / f / wherever they come in a word. Can you find any exceptions to this rule in the following words?

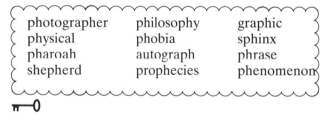

photographer	philosophy	graphic
physical	phobia	sphinx
pharoah	autograph	phrase
shepherd	prophecies	phenomenon

π—0

2 **T.11.3.A.** Listen and repeat the words. Pay attention to your pronunciation of *ph*.

3 Write some sentences with as many / f / sounds in them as you can, like these:

Fred took a photo of his wife feeding the elephant.

François the French chef had an unfortunate fear of frogs.

The pharoah laughed and asked the sphinx to rephrase her frightening prophecy.

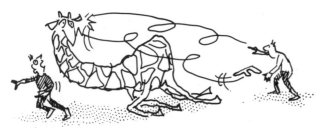

Fifi the giraffe fell lifeless at Philip's feet.

The famished wolf followed Ralph through the forest.

4 ┌─────────┐
    │ T.11.3.B. │ Listen, and practise reading these
    └─────────┘
sentences, and your own, aloud.

70

● Word focus

4 Traffic signs and motoring vocabulary

1 Write what each sign means, using the words in the box.

> traffic lights   roundabout
>
> end of dual carriageway
>
> no through road   no entry
>
> hump bridge   slippery road
>
> pedestrian crossing
>
> road-works   cyclists only
>
> no overtaking   crossroads
>
> quayside or river bank
>
> no U-turns   no motor vehicles

a. *no overtaking*

b. _____

c. _____

d. _____

e. _____

f. ![sign] _____

g. ![sign] _____

h. ![sign] _____

i. ![sign] _____

j. ![sign] _____

k. ![sign] _____

l. ![sign] _____

m. ![sign] _____

n. ![sign] _____

o. ![sign] _____

2 **T.11.4.** Listen and check your answers.

3 Listen again and repeat. Make sure you pronounce the motoring vocabulary correctly.

4 Here are some of the words you have just practised in phonemic script. Transcribe them.

   a. / 'kiː saɪd / _____

   b. / 'saɪklɪsts / _____

   c. / 'træfɪk / _____

   d. / 'vɪəklz / _____

   e. / 'djuːəl / _____

   f. / 'kærɪdʒweɪ / _____

   g. / pəˈdestrɪən / _____

● Connected speech

Do this exercise after the exercise on sentence combination on page 96 of the Student's Book.

5 Sentence dictation

1 **T.11.5.** You will hear each of the following sentences said in two different ways. When you hear the tone, stop the tape and write each sentence, using punctuation to show the differences.

   1. she got a lovely present from her aunt who lives in canada

      a. _____

      b. _____

   2. the taxi driver said the cyclist was the cause of the accident

      a. _____

      b. _____

   3. the cassette recorder which we bought last year was stolen

      a. _____

      b. _____

   4. please don't come here again for my sake

      a. _____

      b. _____

   5. the workers who asked for a pay rise were sacked

      a. _____

      b. _____

2 Work in pairs. Discuss the difference in meaning between the a and b sentences.

6 Third conditional

1 **T.11.6.** Listen and write in the box on the left the number of words you hear in each sentence. (*hadn't* = two words)

a. [12] _____ skidded if _____ icy.

b. [ ] _____ faster, _____ killed.

c. [ ] _____ afforded it _____ credit card.

d. [ ] _____ searched _____ _____ the jewels.

e. [ ] _____ perfect _____ engine _____ .

f. [ ] _____ plane, _____ simpler.

g. [ ] _____ crashed _____ braked suddenly.

h. [ ] _____ to happen, _____ gone.

🔑

2 Listen again and fill in the missing words.

🔑

3 How are these words pronounced when they come in the middle of sentences?

> would have   wouldn't have
> might have   might not have
> could have   couldn't have

🔑

Listen again and repeat the sentences, paying attention to the pronunciation of these words.

4 Choose four of these sentences, and put them into a story. You shouldn't change any of the words, and your story should be 80–100 words long.

🔑

5 Read your story aloud.

● Stress and intonation

7 Surprise tag questions

1 The usual pattern for question tags is:

POSITIVE SENTENCE + NEGATIVE TAG
You're a teacher, aren't you?

NEGATIVE SENTENCE + POSITIVE TAG
You aren't a writer, are you?

But sometimes, when we want to show surprise or annoyance at something we've just heard or just realized, the pattern changes.

POSITIVE SENTENCE + POSITIVE TAG

You're a millionaire, are you?

I'm an oddball, am I?

The intonation always goes up at the end in surprised/annoyed tag questions.

Brian and Alex are chatting at a party.

Fill in the surprised/annoyed tag questions in their dialogue:

A Hello, Brian. Celia's just over there. Let me introduce you.
B Don't worry, Alex, Celia and I already know each other, actually.

A Oh! So you've met my wife before,
(a) _____ ?
B Well yes, actually. We were at Cambridge together.

A Oh! you were at King's College too,
(b) _____ ?
B Yes, in actual fact, I was. We had rooms on the same staircase.

A Ah! So you knew each other quite well, (c) _____?

B Oh, yes, quite well. We saw each other almost every day.

A Ah! So she was a close friend of yours, (d) _____?

B You could say that . . . but then, just before her final exams, she disappeared.

A Oh! She ran off and left you, (e) _____?

B Not just me – Cambridge, her exams, everything! Then one day I got the wedding invite from the south of France.

A And that surprised you, (f) _____?

B Not really. Celia's always been a bit like that – unpredictable!

A Oh! She has, (g) _____?

B Yes. Ever since I first met her. Anyway, Alex, let me be the first to congratulate you!

A Oh! You're pleased about it, (h) _____?

B Of course. You're the one that's going to suffer now.

A Oh! I am, (i) _____?

B Oh, yes. You'll soon wish you'd never laid eyes on San Tropez!
(Celia joins them.)

C Alex, darling, I was just wondering . . . Good Lord! It's Brian Fortescue!

B Ah, so you still remember me, (j) _____?

2 **T.11.7.A.** Listen and check your answers.

3 Listen again. This time say the surprised/annoyed tag questions with the tape, paying attention to your intonation, like this:

You've met my wife before, have you?

At the start of the conversation Alex is politely surprised, but he becomes very annoyed by the end of it. Can you do the same?

4 **T.11.7.B.** Listen and respond with surprised/annoyed question tags. Try to show surprise or annoyance in your intonation.

You know me.   Oh, I do, do I?   Oh, I do, do I?

You listen   *You speak*   *You listen*

5 Work in threes. Act out the dialogue between Alex, Brian, and Celia.

8 Emphatic forms

1 In ordinary speech we often use contractions:

I'm surprised.
I've got a sore throat.
She'll be disappointed.

Sometimes, when we want to give extra emphasis, we use full forms instead of contractions:

I *am* surprised!
I *have* got a sore throat!
She *will* be disappointed!

In some cases, where there is no auxiliary verb, we use the verb *do* to give emphasis:

Do have a drink!
I *did* tell her before she came!

Write in the emphatic forms of the following sentences.

a. Come in. _____

b. I hope she gets better soon. _____

c. I've missed you. _____

d. You promised. _____

e. I'd be grateful. _____

f. I'm sorry. _____

g. Help yourself. _____

h. I warned her. _____

i. He'll be pleased. _____

j. Hurry up. _____

2 **T.11.8.A.** Listen and check your answers.

3 Listen again and practise saying the emphatic forms. Make sure you stress the auxiliary verbs.

4 Complete these dialogues using the expressions you've practised.

a. **A** Oh, I'm going to be late. I'll miss the plane!
    B Shall I drive you to the airport?

    A Oh, _____ .

b. **C** Bad news, is it?
    D Yes, I'm afraid so. My grandmother died last weekend.

    C Oh, _____ .

c. **E** Which film shall we go and see then?
    F Well, actually darling, I'm feeling rather tired. Can't we make it tomorrow night instead?

    E Oh, Frank, _____ .

d. **G** Come on! We should've left ten minutes ago!
    H Don't rush me! Now where did I put my nail varnish?

    G Helen, _____ .

e. **I** Jane, that was splendid!
    J Oh, Ian, did you really like it?
    I Of course! The sauce was delicious. Really delicious.
    J There's some more left if you're still feeling hungry.

    _____ .

f. **K** Mrs Laker, I'm from Pricewise, and this is your lucky day!
    L You what?
    K Your husband has just won £1,000 in the Pricewise Prize Draw!

    L My Eric! Has he really? Oh, _____ .

5 **T.11.8.B.** Listen and check your answers.
   ⊓—0

6 Work in pairs. Choose one of the dialogues. Listen to it again and repeat it. Make sure your intonation and stress is the same. Then act it out without the book.

74

● **Everyday English**

9 Abbreviations

1 What do the following abbreviations stand for?

a. AD   *Anno Domini – The year of Our Lord*

b. AIDS   _____

c. BBC   _____

d. BC   _____

e. EC   _____

f. IQ   _____

g. UK   _____

h. MBE   _____

i. MOT   _____

j. MP   _____

k. UEFA   _____

l. PM   _____

m. RAF   _____

n. UN   _____

o. US   _____

p. USSR   _____

q. VAT   _____

⊓—0

2 **T.11.9.A.** Listen and repeat the abbreviations.

3   Fill in the gaps using the abbreviations you've practised.

'And here, once again, are the news headlines:

'Geoffrey Bowman, former Conservative _____ ,

has been awarded the _____ for his services to literature, in the New Year's Honours List.

'A _____ spokesman today announced that unless there is a marked reduction in British soccer fan

violence _____ teams will be banned from playing in Europe again this season.

'A new _____ test is to be brought in next year, in order to bring British motoring safety standards into

line with those in other _____ countries.

'A team of medical experts from the _____ left for Moscow today in an attempt to control the growing

problem of _____ in the _____ .

'No one has yet claimed responsibility for last night's National Museum bombing. Although no one was injured in the blast, the National's priceless collection of

classical sculpture dating from 400 _____ to

100 _____ has been seriously damaged.

'And that is the end of the one o'clock news.'

4   **T.11.9.B.** Listen and check your answers.
    ᴨ—0

5   Make up some more news stories using the following abbreviations. Use a dictionary to help you.

UFO	CIA	KGB	HMS	RSPCA
NATO	TUC	OPEC	IBM	YMCA
ITN	OXFAM			

6   Work in pairs. **Student A**, read out your news stories. Instead of saying the abbreviations, say fruit or vegetable names. **Student B**, guess what the abbreviations are.

    A The *banana* has called an emergency meeting to discuss the problems of the miners' strike.
    B Is that the TUC?

UNIT 12

● Sounds and spelling

1 The sounds / æ / and / e /
ⒹⒽⒾ

1 **T.12.1.A.** Listen and circle the words you hear.

a. pan   pen
b. man   men
c. sad   said
d. salary   celery
e. landing   lending

π—0

2 Practise saying the sounds.

To make the sound / æ / your mouth should be open like this, and your tongue should be **down** at the **front** of your mouth:

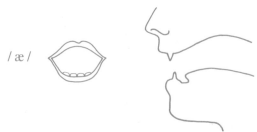

/ æ /

To make the sound / e / your mouth should be less open, and your tongue should be a little **higher** and further **forward**:

/ e /

3 **T.12.1.B.** Listen to these pairs of words, and repeat them.

/ æ /	/ e /
pan	pen
man	men
sad	said
salary	celery
landing	lending
band	bend
flash	flesh
tan	ten

4 **T.12.1.C.** Listen and fill in the boxes.

	1	2	3	4
A				
B				
C				
D				

π—0

5 Now work with a partner. Make your own box dictation with / æ / and / e / words. Here are some more pairs you can use. Remember you can use each word more than once.

bat – bet	cattle – kettle	jam – gem
sat – set	mansion – mention	pat – pet
had – head	bag – beg	sand – send
ham – hem	marry – merry	pack – peck

	1	2	3
A			
B			
C			
D			

You

	1	2	3
A			
B			
C			
D			

Your partner

2 Rhyming words

1 Choose a word from the box below which rhymes with the following words.

a. rhyme *climb*

b. half _____

c. write _____

d. sword _____

e. knee _____

f. wreck _____

g. limb _____

h. know _____

i. who _____

j. plant _____

k. rustle _____

l. funny _____

m. farm _____

n. bet _____

o. smile _____

p. diet _____

climb	money	debt	hymn
gnawed	aunt	though	cheque
muscle	through	laugh	quay
knight	quiet	psalm	aisle

2 **T.12.2.A.** Listen and check your answers.
π—0

3 Listen again and repeat. Make sure you pronounce the vowel sounds correctly. Take care you **don't** pronounce the silent letters!

4 Fill the gaps in each sentence with a rhyming pair.

a. The dragon *gnawed* St. George's *sword*.

b. I gave my _____ a lovely _____.

c. He signed a _____ to buy the _____.

d. If you're in _____, you

shouldn't _____.

e. The bridegroom's _____

shone down the _____.

f. We'll never _____ who wrote

it, _____.

g. I strained each _____ to sing

the _____.

h. Please put me _____ to you-

know-_____.

5 **T.12.2.B.** Listen and check your answers.
π—0

6 Listen again and practise saying the sentences with the correct rhythm.

● · ● · ● · ● ● · ● · ● · ● · ●

3 Silent letters

1 All these words contain letters which are not pronounced. Cross out the unpronounced letters.

a. han̸dkerchief

b. muscle

c. aisle

d. condemn

e. Wednesday

f. biscuit

g. phlegm

h. island

i. sandwich

j. hymn

k. circuit

l. leopard

m. Thames

n. autumn

o. buoy

p. corps

q. solemn

r. Leicester

s. handsome

t. ironing

u. bruise

π—0

2 **T.12.3.A.** Listen and practise saying the words with the correct pronunciation. Keep the silent letters silent!

3 **T.12.3.B.** Listen to a foreign student mispronouncing some of these words. Respond to what she says by echoing her words – but *not* her pronunciation.

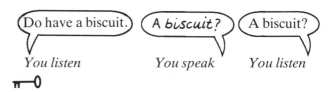

Do have a biscuit.   A *biscuit*?   A biscuit?

You listen   *You speak*   *You listen*

π—0

● Word focus

4 Stress in multi-word verbs and nouns

1 Use the following multi-word nouns and their verb forms to fill the gaps in the following pairs of sentences. Remember that the noun and the verb often have different meanings. You will probably need to check some of the words in your dictionary.

break-in	fall-out	sell-out
make-up	takeoff	lookout
send-off	drop-out	
breakdown	comeback	

a. They've had another *break-in* next door. Fortunately nothing very much was stolen this time.

Did they *break in* through the back window, then?

b. Keep a _____ for a parking space, will you?

_____ for pickpockets!

c. She had a nervous _____ last year and had to give up her job.

I hope our car doesn't _____ again.

d. I'd rather you didn't use my _____ ! You left the top off the mascara and it's all dried up now.

Don't let's argue, darling. Let's kiss and

_____ , shall we?

e. He's a university _____ , you know. He left after only two years.

She wants to _____ of the play. She says she's had enough.

f. If ever there's a nuclear war, more people will die

from radioactive _____ than from the explosion.

I don't want to _____ with you. I hate arguments.

g. He does a wonderful _____ of Margaret Thatcher. He sounds just like her.

Is the plane going to _____ soon?

h. We gave the newlyweds a fantastic

_____ —champagne, cake, tin cans tied to the car! It was perfect.

This summer school in Rome looks interesting. I

think I'll _____ for a brochure.

i. The Michael Jackson concert was a complete

_____ . There wasn't a single ticket left.

I'm sure we'll _____ of these cards before Christmas, and we won't be able to order any more before the New Year.

j. This was the year that 1950's heart-throb, Bart

Pontoni, made his _____ .

Goodbye Arthur. I'm leaving. Maybe one day I'll

_____ to you, but don't count on it!

2 **T.12.4.** Listen and check your answers.

3 Listen again and mark the stress in the multi-word nouns and verbs.

    ●   ●
a break-in   to break in

What do you notice about the stress in multi-word nouns, and the stress in multi-word verbs?

4 Listen to the sentences again and repeat. Make sure you stress the multi-word nouns and verbs correctly.

● Connected speech

5 Sentences with and without the indefinite article

1 **T.12.5.A.** Listen and tick (✓) the sentences you hear.

1. That's a very expensive paper.
2. That's very expensive paper.

3. There's a Mr Jones here to see you, sir.
4. There's Mr Jones here to see you, sir.

5. This is quite a dark wood.
6. This is quite dark wood.

7. What a nice lamb!
8. What nice lamb!

9. I've got a few friends here.
10. I've got few friends here.

11. I'm sure she's a cleaner.
12. I'm sure she's cleaner.

13. I met such a friendly policeman in London.
14. I met such friendly policemen in London.

15. This novel is about a man's search for freedom.
16. This novel is about man's search for freedom.

⊞—O

2 Read all the sentences aloud.

3 Match each sentence above with one of the following responses.

a. [1] Yes, but I like reading *The Times*.

b. [ ] Yes, I wonder if we'll ever find our way out.

c. [ ] Yes, she doesn't look as dirty as before.

d. [ ] Not again! What does he want this time?

e. [ ] Mmm. Isn't it delicious?

f. [ ] Yes, he was born only a few days ago.

g. [ ] Oh, she can't earn much doing that.

h. [ ] Was he on duty at the time?

i. [ ] Well, you make friends wherever you go, don't you?

j. [ ] Yes, but I don't like cheap stationery.

k. [ ] Mr who? Oh, say I'm in a meeting, Sandra, and find out what he wants.

l. [ ] Oh dear, you poor thing. You must be lonely.

m. [ ] Yes, the whole dining room suite is made of mahogany.

n. [ ] And what about woman's search for freedom, too?

o. [ ] Yes, I think they're less aggressive because they don't usually carry guns.

p. [ ] And his wife's attempts to help him in that search, surely?

⊞—O

4 Work in pairs. **Student A** read a sentence from exercise 1 aloud. **Student B** reply with the appropriate response from exercise 3.

6 Word linking

1 [T.12.6.] Listen and mark the different kinds of word-linking in the following graffiti, like this:

/ j /   / j /
Today is the first day of the rest of your life . . .
/ j /
enjoy it!
/ g /   / p /   / k /
Lord give me patience – but make it quick!

⊞—O

2 Listen again and repeat. Make sure you link the words correctly.

● Stress and intonation

7 Exclamations

1 Match up each of the following adjectives with its opposite in the box below.

disgusting *delicious*   warm _____

cruel _____   smart _____

ugly _____   lovely _____

sensible _____   cheerful _____

stale _____   important _____

cheap _____   varied _____

delicious	cold	fresh	insignificant
monotonous	horrible	foolish	shabby
depressing	kind	expensive	attractive

2 [T.12.7.A.] Listen and check your answers.

3 Listen again and practise saying the words.

4 Fill in the grid of countable and uncountable nouns. Use the anagrams to help you.

General (uncountable)	Particular (countable)	
food	*meal*	LEMA
clothes		SRESD
advice		NITEGUSOGS
bread		ALFO
luggage		SEAC
rubbish		SEMS
music		UNTE
people		NESROP
work		BOJ
information		LETIDA
weather		ELITMAC
furniture		FOAS

5 Transform the following sentences, using a countable noun instead of an uncountable noun.

What delicious food!

What *a delicious meal* !

What lovely clothes!

What _____ !

What varied work!

What _____ !

6 [T.12.7.B.] Listen and check your answers.

7 Listen again and repeat. Make sure your voice rises and falls like this.

What delicious food!

What a delicious meal!

8 [T.12.7.C.] Listen and respond.

sensible advice | *What sensible advice!* | What sensible advice!

You listen | *You speak* | *You listen*

80

8 Stress patterns in words and sentences

1 The following words come from the questionnaire on pages 99–100 of the Student's Book. Can you put them into the correct columns according to stress?

Superman	Cinderella	philosophy	demanding
efficient	compulsive	abilities	rehearsal
unbearable	batteries	efficiently	management
habitat	certainly	occupation	enjoyable
achiever	distracted	everything	creative
happening	energetic	copyright	excuses

● • •	• ● •
Superman	*demanding*

• ● • •	• • ● •
philosophy	*Cinderella*

2 **T.12.8.A.** Listen and check your answers.

Listen again and repeat the words. Make sure you stress them correctly.

3 Sort out the following lines to make two separate poems. (One is called 'Superman' and the other is 'Cinderella'.) The rhythm and rhymes should help. Letter them S and C .

Hello there, Superman. S

Are you crying, Cinderella? C

Don't be sorry,

I've got a telegram

Here's your chance:

With my magic

Wishing you Happy Returns of the day!

And there's some kryptonite

And your pumpkin

Here in this parcel, so

Now you're defenceless, and can't run away.

You will make it to the dance.

4 **T.12.8.B.** Listen and check your answers.

Listen again and repeat the two poems. Make sure you stress them correctly and say them rhythmically.

5 **T.12.8.C.** Listen to the following poems and mark the stress.

       ●   ●
    Aladdin was lazy.

    He never would learn.

    But now he's a rich man

    With money to burn.

    Sir Lancelot

    Loved Guinevere.

    He blushed a lot

    When she was near.

🔑—0

6 Listen again and read the poems aloud. Make sure you stress them correctly and say them rhythmically.

● Everyday English

9 Famous buildings, monuments, books, and works of art

1 Look at the buildings and monuments listed below. Write in 'the' where it is necessary.

a. _the_ Colosseum

b. _____ Buckingham Palace

c. _____ Eiffel Tower

d. _____ Statue of Liberty

e. _____ Nelson's Column

f. _____ Pyramids

g. _____ Sphinx

h. _____ Victoria and Albert Museum

i. _____ Taj Mahal

j. _____ St. Paul's Cathedral

k. _____ Sistine Chapel

l. _____ Westminster Abbey

2 **T.12.9.A.** Listen and check your answers.
🔑—0

3 Listen again and repeat. Make sure you pronounce all the names the English way.

4 Look at the books and works of art listed below. Cross out *the* where it is not necessary.

a. ~~the~~ *Das Kapital*

b. the *Bible*

c. the *Odyssey*

d. the *King Lear*

e. the Bayeux Tapestry

f. the Mona Lisa

g. the Venus de Milo

h. the *Paradise Lost*

i. the Michelangelo's David

j. the *Godfather*

k. the *Don Quixote*

l. the *Koran*

5 **T.12.9.B.** Listen and check your answers.
🔑—0

6 Listen again and repeat. Make sure you pronounce all the names the English way.

7 Fill in the gaps.

a.   *Das Kapital*   was written by Karl Marx.

b. _____ is one of Shakespeare's great tragedies.

c. _____ was built to honour a great British admiral.

d. _____ was presented to newly independent North America by the Republic of France.

e. _____ was painted by Leonardo da Vinci

f. _____ is to Muslims what _____ is to Christians.

g. _____ was woven to commemorate the invasion of England by William of Normandy in 1066.

h. _____ ceiling was painted by Michelangelo.

i. _____ was designed by Sir Christopher Wren.

j. Many early Christian martyrs were thrown to the lions in _____ .

🔑—0

KEY

THE PHONEMIC ALPHABET

Vowels and diphthongs

1. /iː/   s<u>ee</u>   /siː/
2. /ɪ/   s<u>i</u>t   /sɪt/
3. /e/   t<u>e</u>n   /ten/
4. /æ/   h<u>a</u>t   /hæt/
5. /ɑː/   <u>ar</u>m   /ɑːm/
6. /ɒ/   g<u>o</u>t   /gɒt/
7. /ɔː/   s<u>aw</u>   /sɔː/
8. /ʊ/   p<u>u</u>t   /pʊt/
9. /uː/   t<u>oo</u>   /tuː/
10. /ʌ/   c<u>u</u>p   /kʌp/
11. /ɜː/   f<u>ur</u>   /fɜː/
12. /ə/   <u>a</u>go   /əˈgəʊ/
13. /eɪ/   p<u>a</u>ge   /peɪdʒ/
14. /əʊ/   h<u>o</u>me   /həʊm/
15. /aɪ/   f<u>i</u>ve   /faɪv/
16. /aʊ/   n<u>ow</u>   /naʊ/
17. /ɔɪ/   j<u>oi</u>n   /dʒɔɪn/
18. /ɪə/   n<u>ea</u>r   /nɪə/
19. /eə/   h<u>air</u>   /heə/
20. /ʊə/   p<u>ure</u>   /pjʊə/

Consonants

1. /p/   <u>p</u>en   /pen/
2. /b/   <u>b</u>ad   /bæd/
3. /t/   <u>t</u>ea   /tiː/
4. /d/   <u>d</u>id   /dɪd/
5. /k/   <u>c</u>at   /kæt/
6. /g/   <u>g</u>ot   /gɒt/
7. /tʃ/   <u>ch</u>in   /tʃɪn/
8. /dʒ/   <u>J</u>une   /dʒuːn/
9. /f/   <u>f</u>all   /fɔːl/
10. /v/   <u>v</u>oice   /vɔɪs/
11. /θ/   <u>th</u>in   /θɪn/
12. /ð/   <u>th</u>en   /ðen/
13. /s/   <u>s</u>o   /səʊ/
14. /z/   <u>z</u>oo   /zuː/
15. /ʃ/   <u>sh</u>e   /ʃiː/
16. /ʒ/   vi<u>s</u>ion   /ˈvɪʒən/
17. /h/   <u>h</u>ow   /haʊ/
18. /m/   <u>m</u>an   /mæn/
19. /n/   <u>n</u>o   /nəʊ/
20. /ŋ/   si<u>ng</u>   /sɪŋ/
21. /l/   <u>l</u>eg   /leg/
22. /r/   <u>r</u>ed   /red/
23. /j/   <u>y</u>es   /jes/
24. /w/   <u>w</u>et   /wet/

1 Vowels (1)

3.
a.	pot	i.	feel
b.	bill	j.	seat
c.	door	k.	sick
d.	tea	l.	bought
e.	Scot	m.	wool
f.	pull	n.	true
g.	food	o.	sort
h.	who	p.	could

4.   **T.0.1.B.**

a. /ɒ/	e. /iː/	i. /ʊ/
b. /ʊ/	f. /ɔː/	j. /ɔː/
c. /iː/	g. /ɪ/	k. /ɪ/
d. /u:/	h. /uː/	l. /ɒ/

2 Vowels (2)

2.
a. nurse	f. worker
b. butler	g. dancer
c. actor	h. plumber
d. actress	i. secretary
e. farmer	j. barman

3.   **T.0.2.B.**

1.	bell	c.	4.	purse	a.
	bull	b.		puss	d.
	bill	a.		pass	b.
	ball	d.		piece	c.
2.	fool	c.	5.	fist	c.
	full	d.		fast	b.
	fell	b.		first	d.
	fall	a.		feast	a.
3.	hat	c.	6.	cot	c.
	hut	d.		court	a.
	hurt	b.		cat	b.
	heart	a.		cut	d.

3 Consonants

5.   **T.0.3.C.**

1.	b.	5.	d.
2.	a.	6.	b.
3.	d.	7.	a.
4.	c.	8.	b.

4 Diphthongs (1)

3.
a. boy	j. child
b. wave	k. wages
c. hide	l. shout
d. day	m. choice
e. how	n. shy
f. write/right	o. danger
g. found	p. enjoyed
h. boiling	q. either
i. they	r. shower

5 Diphthongs (2)

3.   **T.0.5.B.**

1.	b.	7.	b.
2.	b.	8.	a.
3.	a.	9.	b.
4.	a.	10.	a.
5.	b.	11.	b.
6.	b.	12.	a.

4.
1.	a. pay	7.	a. die
2.	a. race	8.	b. bare/bear
3.	b. grey	9.	a. tour
4.	b. cow	10.	b. note
5.	a. bowl	11.	a. dare
6.	a. load	12.	b. fear

6 Revision

2.   **T.0.6.**

a. /feɪs/		n. /hænd/	
b. /aɪz/		o. /θʌm/	
c. /ɪəz/		p. /ˈfɪŋgə/	
d. /nəʊz/		q. /tʃest/	
e. /tʃiːks/		r. /weɪst/	
f. /maʊθ/		s. /hɪps/	
g. /tiːθ/		t. /ˈbɒtəm/	
h. /tʌŋ/		u. /θaɪ/	
i. /tʃɪn/		v. /niː/	
j. /dʒɔː/		w. /ʃɪn/	
k. /ˈʃəʊldə/		x. /ˈæŋkl/	
l. /ɑːm/		y. /fʊt/	
m. /ˈelbəʊ/			

UNIT 1

1

1 **T.1.1.A.**

Well, of course Chaucer was writing in the 14th century, and the English he used was very different from our modern English in terms of pronunciation. I suppose it was basically more phonetic. I mean, you pronounced all the words as they were written. So, for example, 'knight' was pronounced / knɪxt / – sounding the letters 'k' and 'gh', which of course are silent in modern English. The word 'time' is another example of this rule. You see that would have been / ti: mə / in Chaucer's day – with the final 'e' sounded. It was all more logical really – 'was' was / wæs /, 'worthy' was / wuːɹðɪ /, and 'began' was spelt with an 'i' rather than an 'e'.

Sometimes, of course, the grammar was a bit different, as well as the pronunciation – to / ɹiː dən /, for example, instead of 'to ride'. And then of course there are clear differences in the way some words were stressed. 'Chivalry' in modern English was / tʃɪvælˈriː jə / – with the stress towards the end of the word – in Chaucer's day. The same with / ɒˈnuː ɹ / or 'honour' as we'd say it nowadays.

All in all, although Chaucer's English looks reasonably familiar on the printed page, it must have sounded very different from modern English when read aloud.

A (knight) ther (was) and that a (worthy) man
That, fro the (time) that he first (bigan)
To (riden) out, he loved (chivalrye)
Trouthe and (honour), fredom and curteisye.

2

2 **T.1.1.B.**

/iː/
a. fr**ee**

/ɪ/
b. b**e**gan

/aɪ/
c. t**i**me

/iː/
d. sp**ea**k

/aɪ/
e. dr**i**ed

/iː/
f. p**eo**ple

/aɪ//ɪ/
g. b**i**l**i**ngual

/iː/
h. r**e**cent

/aɪ/
i. w**i**despread

/ɪ/
j. b**u**siness

/ɪ/
k. lang**ua**ge

/ɪ/ /ɪ/
l. p**i**dg**i**n

2

1 **T.1.2.A.**

A /ɪ/ /æ/ /ɒ/ /e/ /ʌ/
B /aɪ/ /eɪ/ /əʊ/ /iː/ /juː/

4	*-ing*	*-ed*
	spitting	moped
	winning	whipped
	coping	noted
	shopping	popped

	-er	*-est*
	fitter	closest
	cuter	thinnest
	fatter	maddest
	paler	saddest

3

1. noun	9. punctuation
2. verb	10. preposition
3. vowel	11. pronunciation
4. tense	12. consonant
5. regular	13. auxiliary
6. irregular	14. adjective
7. singular	15. intonation
8. plural	

4

4 **T.1.4.B.**

● /ə/	●/ə/
industry	politics
● /ə/	/ə/●/ə/
industrial	political
● /ə/	/ə/●/ə/
industrialist	politician
● /ə/	/ə/●
industrialize	politicize
● /ə/	●/ə/
invention	nation
●	/ə/●
inventive	nationalistic
● /ə/	● /ə/
inventor	nationalist
●	● /ə/
invent	nationalize
/ə/●/ə/	●/ə/
competition	analysis
/ə/ ●/ə/	/ə/● /ə/
competitive	analytical
/ə/ ● /ə/	● /ə/
competitor	analyst
/ə/ ●	●/ə/
compete	analyse
● /ə/	
criticism	
● /ə/	
critical	
●	
critic	
●	
criticize	

5

1 **T.1.5.**

a. Present Simple (active)
b. Past Continuous (active)
c. Present Continuous (active)
d. Present Continuous (passive)
e. Past Simple (passive)
f. Present Perfect Continuous (active)
g. Present Continuous (active)
h. Present Perfect Simple (passive)
i. Past Continuous (passive)
j. Future Perfect (active)
k. Present Perfect Continuous (active)
l. Future Continuous (active)

2 a. Do you come here a lot?
   b. They weren't expecting us.
   c. They're having another argument.
   d. The car's being mended at the moment.
   e. This letter was posted two months ago.
   f. That's been annoying me all day.
   g. We're just trying to help.
   h. We haven't been told anything yet.
   i. I'm sure we were being followed just then.
   j. I'll have gone home by eight o'clock.
   k. They've been having a lot of problems lately.
   l. We'll be waiting for you at the entrance.

3 The main verb is stressed in each case, and the auxiliary verbs are unstressed and pronounced in their weak forms.

7

2 T.1.7.B.

   1. *   3. **   5. **
   2. ***   4. ***   6. *

8

1 T.1.8.A.

   Question words, verbs, and nouns are stressed.

2 T.1.8.B.

   a. Have you got any children?
   b. Are you married?
   c. Do you speak any other languages?
   d. Do you do any sports?

---

3 Here the *Wh-* questions start high and have a falling intonation. The *Yes/No* questions do not start so high and they rise up a little at the end. This is a very common pattern in English, but it is not the only one.

5 T.1.8.D.

   a. Where were you born?
   b. Which countries have you been to?
   c. What's your job?
   d. Why are you learning English?
   e. How old are you?
   f. When did you get married?

9

1 T.1.9.

   A   B
   bungalow   barbecue
   casino   cuisine
   chalet   hors d'oeuvres
   restaurant   gourmet
   villa

   C
   ballet
   concerto
   karate

10

1 If you just list the *-teen* words – thirteen, fourteen, fifteen etc. – the stress pattern becomes ● ₒ.

2 a. 1170   e. 1815   i. 1713
   b. 1216   f. 1516   j. 1540
   c. 1790   g. 1450   k. 1930
   d. 1830   h. 1618   l. 1980

---

3 T.1.10.C.

   a. There were thirteen guests at the dinner table.
   b. He's just turned nineteen.
   c. The box contained sixteen toy soldiers.
   d. Two sevens are fourteen.
   e. Seventeen's my lucky number.
   f. I used to smoke at least fifteen cigarettes a day.
   g. She lives at number eighteen.
   h. It weighs exactly fourteen kilos.

4 The stress pattern in *-teen* words is ● ₒ when they are followed by a noun or when they are listed (see 1), and ₒ ● when they are not.

UNIT 2

1

1 T.2.1.A.

   a. What nice clean air!
   b. Will you heat that soup up?
   c. These terrorists can't be armed.
   d. There's something wrong with my hearing.
   e. Do you like eels?

4 T.2.1.C.

a. He's got absolutely no idea /w/
   how /w/ /j/ organize things.
b. It's Harriet's free evening, /j/
   and she's gone to the opera. /j/
c. We aren't going to hurry off /j/ /j/
   to the zoo now after all. /w/
d. Henry and I agree that /j/ /j/
   you are to inherit the antique /w/ /w/ /j/
   hatstand.
e. They admire Hugh a lot. He's /j/ /w/
   a handsome boy and /j/
   so intelligent too. /w/

5 /w/
   /j/

2

1 *hotel* – in modern English the *h*
   is sounded in *hotel*. In the
   other four words the *h* is
   silent.
   perhaps – the *h* is sounded and
   the *r* is silent in *perhaps*. In the
   other four words the *r* is
   sounded and the *h* is silent.
   whole – the *h* is sounded and the
   w is silent in *whole*. In the
   other four words the *w* is
   sounded and the *h* is silent.

2 a. heir, honest, hour, and
      honour
   b. /r/
   c. /w/ . . . /h/

3 yoghurt   exhibition
   harmony   heiress
   vehicle   hierarchy /k/
   cowhide   hospital

   exhaust
/f/ (pharoah
/f/ (philharmonic
   herb (in British English)
   herb (in US English)

3

1 T.2.3.A.

a. This blue and white cup's
   nice.
b. There's a big brown bag in
   the corner.
c. I can't move – I've got a cat
   on my knee.
d. Of course you can use that
   old rug if you want.
e. It's my uncle that's the
   problem.

4 T.2.3.C.

a. The young man was wearing
   fashionable sunglasses, black
   gloves, and a gangster's hat.
b. The wasp that's trapped in
   the jar of blackcurrant jam is
   buzzing angrily.
c. Thank you very much for
   coming to pay back that
   money you borrowed on
   Monday, Danny.
d. While cutting up lamb the
   drunken butcher hacked off
   his thumb with a hatchet.
e. My husband had a double
   brandy, my mother wanted
   apple juice, but I drank
   champagne.

4

1 T.2.4.

/ æ /	/ eɪ /
cracked	traders
accident	danger
family	donated
charity	babies
happened	grateful

/ ə /	/ ɑː /
hospital	disaster
temperature	after
another	father
regular	
ligaments	

/ ɔː /	
falling	all

5

	-ful	-less
pain	painful	painless
beauty	beautiful	—
harm	harmful	harmless
worth	—	worthless
hope	hopeful	hopeless
care	careful	careless
delight	delightful	—
price	—	priceless
help	helpful	helpless
success	successful	—
truth	truthful	—
use	useful	useless
thought	thoughtful	thoughtless
child	—	childless

6

T.2.6.

War and Peace
Out of Africa
Death on the Nile
Alice in Wonderland
The Wizard of Oz
Close Encounters of the Third
   Kind
A Clockwork Orange
Lawrence of Arabia
Cat on a Hot Tin Roof
Kiss of the Spiderwoman
Indiana Jones and the Temple of
   Doom
Venus and Adonis
First Among Equals
Death of a Salesman

7

1 T.2.7.

   a. 11   f. 10
   b. 9   g. 10
   c. 13   h. 7
   d. 8   i. 7
   e. 6   j. 8

2
a. He's worked at the post office since he was 16.
b. Who's eaten the last piece of chocolate cake?
c. She's written lots of postcards to send to her friends in England.
d. We've been studying English for six months.
e. She's never been windsurfing before.
f. He's felt much healthier since he gave up smoking.
g. I've been writing short stories since I left university.
h. Have you ever met anyone from Transylvania?
i. What has he done to your hair?
j. I've been cooking since half past five.

8

2 T.2.8.B.
1. of . . . for
2. at . . . at
3. to . . . from
4. of
5. to . . . for

3 a. 3   c. 1   e. 4
b. 5   d. 2

9

1 T.2.9.A.
a. d   c. h   e. d
b. h   d. d   f. h

2 The first sentence shows definite agreement, the second shows hesitant agreement.

3 T.2.9.B.
A Didn't Harry star in a musical recently?
B Yes, I think he did. (d)
A I thought so. Wasn't it *Cats*?
B Yes, I believe it was. (d)
A Now, the question is: would he be interested in another musical so soon?
B I don't know. I imagine he would be. (h)
A Well, is he doing anything at the National Theatre this season?
B No, I don't think he is. (h)
A Right! So he'll be free next summer – just when we need him.
B Yes, I presume he will be. (h)
A Hmm. Isn't Harry's nephew in the Royal Shakespeare Company too?
B Yes, I believe he is. (d)
A Well, couldn't we audition him for the part of young David? That way we'd solve all our casting problems.

10

2 T.2.10.B.
1. gear   9. rays
2. heir   10. axis
3. jeer   11. crash
4. risky   12. wreck
5. sick   13. jazz
6. crisis   14. wager
7. scary   15. whisker
8. exercise 16. crazy

UNIT 3

1

1 T.3.1.A.
a. ran   f. win
b. rang   g. sing
c. rank   h. sung
d. thin   i. bunk
e. pink   j. banger

4 T.3.1.B.
a. Aunt Angela banged her ankle while dancing a tango with Uncle Frank at a Birmingham skating rink.
b. The Hong Kong gangster, drinking a gin sling in a singles' bar, winked at the pretty, young singer singing romantic songs.
c. What's that long, pink, stringy thing on Angus King's tongue?
d. A Singapore dancer was wrongfully hanged for killing a Washington banker outside a boxing ring.

5 T.3.1.C.

/ ŋə /	/ ŋgə /
singer	anger
coathanger	ironmonger
left-winger	hunger
bellringer	finger
banger	linger

/ ndʒə /
stranger
plunger
challenger
danger
ginger

2

2 T.3.2.A.

When *r* comes before the vowel sound in the syllable it is pronounced in both American and British English.

When *r* comes after the vowel sound in the syllable it is pronounced in American English, but not in British English.

3

1 T.3.3.A.

profession completion

fashion option

question instruction

solution occupation

promotion emotion

conclusion communication

The stress is always on the next to last syllable. -ion is pronounced / ən / in English.

3

short	long
a	
/ æ /	/ eɪ /
fashion	occupation
	communication
e	
/ e /	/ iː /
profession	completion
question	
o	
/ ɒ /	/ əʊ /
option	promotion
	emotion
u	
/ ʌ /	/ uː /
instruction	conclusion
	solution

If there is one consonant between the stressed syllable and the -ion suffix, then the vowel sound is long.
If there are two or more consonants between the stressed syllable and the -ion suffix, then the vowel sound is short.

4

T.3.4.

pay rise (n.) promotion (n.)
salary (n.) overtime (n.)
application (n.) shifts (n.)
career (n.) wages (n.)
sack (v.)/(n.) training (n.)
degree (n.) qualified (a.)
retire (v.) redundant (a.)

5

1 T.3.5.A.

a. comma
b. full stop
c. question mark
d. exclamation mark
e. colon
f. semi-colon
g. apostrophe
h. inverted commas
i. hyphen
j. dash

2 T.3.5.D.

Alice hates her job. She works in a drab office with bare walls, and the work conditions are unsafe. The people where she works don't like her, and she always feels as if they are picking on her. She hates the work, too, because she thinks of it as dead-end work that is not important anyway.

Cynthia likes her job. Her desk is the brightest spot in the building, and her section got last year's safety award. The people she works with are always giving parties or doing things for each other, and she thinks of them as friends rather than co-workers. The job itself is not an important one, but Cynthia says it is a small part of an important company, and she intends to move up in the company.

The funny thing is that Alice and Cynthia work for the same company and have the same job title. But Cynthia knows a secret: a worker who takes responsibility for her job can make it better.

6

1 T.3.6.A.

The *r* at the end of *over-* **is** pronounced when the word (or syllable) that follows begins with a vowel. It is not pronounced when the word (or syllable) afterwards begins with a consonant sound.

3 T.3.6.B.

M Peter! Are you going anywhere over Easter this year?
P Well, yes, as a matter of fact we are. We're off on a tour of Italy for a week or two.
M Mmm. That sounds really wonderful. Where exactly will you be going?
P Oh, here and there. Rome's more or less definite, but apart from that we're open to suggestion.
M Are you travelling by coach?
P No, by car, actually.
M Dear old Italy! When you're in Rome you must remember to throw a coin over your shoulder into the Trevi fountain.
P Really? What for?
M Well, if you do that, it means that, sooner or later, you're sure to return.

7

1 T.3.7.

a. gone   c. mother

b. California   d. my

2 The word is stressed in each case to correct the mistake made in the question.

4 Possible answers:
a. – Have you found fifty
pounds?
– Have you lost fifteen
pounds?
– Have you lost fifty dollars?
– Has John lost fifty pounds?
b. – Has your sister broken her
arm?
– Has your sister cut her leg?
– Has your cousin broken her
leg?
– Has Ann's sister broken her
leg?
c. – Have the Smiths bought a
flat in London?
– Have the Baileys rented a
flat in London?
– Have the Baileys bought a
house in London?
– Have the Baileys bought a
flat in Birmingham?

8

1 ┌─────────┐
  │ T.3.8.A. │
  └─────────┘

A I think I want to go to
university.
B So do I.
C Oh, I don't.
D I haven't applied for any jobs
yet.
E No, neither have I.
F Oh, I have.
G I definitely wouldn't enjoy
dealing with money a lot in
my job.
H Nor would I.
I No, me neither.
J Anyway, I think my Dad can
help me to find something
where he works.
K Yeah, so can mine.
L Mine can't.

2 B = a   H = a
  C = d   I = a
  E = a   K = a
  F = d   L = d

3 The pronoun *I* is the most
stressed, because the speaker
wants to emphasize what *he or
she* thinks, not what the first
speaker thinks.
The auxiliary verbs are weak
when they come before the
pronouns so they are
pronounced *do* / də /, *have* / həv /,
and *can* / kən /.

4 ┌─────────┐
  │ T.3.8.B. │
  └─────────┘

A I can type quite well.
B So can I.
A I can't speak any foreign
languages.
B Neither can I.
A I know a little bit about
computers.
B So do I.
A I don't do much travelling in
my present job.
B Neither do I.
A I'm not particularly well paid
either.
B Neither am I.
A I'd like to change jobs quite
soon.
B So would I.
A I've always wanted to work
abroad.
B So have I.
A But I've never really had the
opportunity.
B Neither have I.
A Although I spent some time
living abroad when I was a
student.
B So did I.
A In fact I wish I was a student
again now.
B So do I.

9

1,2 ┌─────────┐
    │ T.3.9.A. │
    └─────────┘

Speaker B's part in the short
dialogues is as follows:
a. Have you?   e. Are you?
b. Did you?   f. Has she?
c. Is she?   g. Can they?
d. Did it?   h. Were they?

2 In dialogues a, c, f, and h,
Speaker **B** is interested in
what Speaker **A** is saying. In
dialogues b, d, e, and g, Speaker
B is uninterested in what
Speaker **A** is saying.

4 ┌─────────┐
  │ T.3.9.B. │
  └─────────┘

Diana's got a new job.
Has she?
Liz and Trevor are getting married.
Are they?
We've got a new kitten.
Have you?
We saw a fantastic film last night.
Did you?
I got a pay rise today!
Did you?
Ian was looking for you.
Was he?
My wife's working in
Los Angeles at the moment.
Is she?
We can get Sky Channel in our
new flat.
Can you?
John would like to come walking
with us on Sunday.
Would he?
I'll be passing the post office later.
Will you?

10

1 ┌────────┐
  │ T.3.10. │
  └────────┘

engineer   biologist

journalist policeman

architect   psychiatrist

choreographer philosopher

photographer secretary

chemist   physicist

2 Possible answers:
a. chemist, biologist,
b. engineer, physicist
c. journalist, psychiatrist
d. choreographer, photographer
e. policeman, secretary

UNIT 4

1

1 | T.4.1.A. |

  a. There's something wrong with this veal.
  b. Look at all those whales!
  c. Now this is an old vine.
  d. I'm sure it's in the west.
  e. Can't you do something about that viper?

4

	1	2	3
A	west	whale	vine
B	veil	vet	west
C	vine	west	wet

| T.4.1.C. |

A What's in box A1?
B Box A1 . . . er . . . *west*.
A What's in A2?
B A2 . . . that's *whale*.
A What about A3?
B *Vine*.
A B1?
B *Veil*.
A Er . . . what about B2?
B B2 . . . *vet*.
A And B3?
B B3 . . . *west*.
A OK . . . Now what's in box C1?
B Box C1 . . . *vine*.
A And box C2?
B Box C2 . . . *west*.
A Aha! And what about box C3? What's in that?
B Box C3 . . . that's *wet*.

2

1 | T.4.2. |

  1. two   8. wrap
  2. wrist   9. write
  3. whole   10. who
  4. wrong   11. wrestler
  5. wreck   12. answer
  6. wrinkle   13. sword
  7. wriggle   14. wreath

3 When *w* comes before the letter *r* or the letters *ho* it is silent. *Two*, *answer*, and *sword* also have silent *w*s.

3

1 | T.4.3. |

Sounded *g*	Silent *g*
ignite	gnome
signature	foreign
recognition	sign
ignorance	gnat
dignified	campaign
ignore	gnaw
ignition	resign
significant	reign
resignation	foreigner

3 When the letters *gn* come at the beginning or the end of a word *g* is silent. Some other words, like *foreigner* for example, also contain silent *g*.

4

1   1. ineffective   9. illegal
  2. indirect   10. irregular
  3. impolite   11. illogical
  4. incurable   12. immoral
  5. insignificant 13. incorrect
  6. irrational   14. imperfect
  7. immature   15. irresponsible
  8. informal   16. insufficient

2 We use *im-* + words beginning with the letters *p* or *m*.
We use *ir-* + words beginning with the letter *r*.
We use *il-* + words beginning with the letter *l*.

5

1 | T.4.5. |

  a. chapter
  b. rhyme
  c. character
  d. hero
  e. scene
  f. author
  g. rhythm
  h. heroine
  i. dialogue
  j. playwright
  k. science fiction
  l. narrator
  m. horror story
  n. poem
  o. autobiography
  p. poet

2 Possible answers:
  a. Jules Verne wrote some wonderful science fiction stories.
  b. The heroine of the book is a girl called Alice.
  c. Anthony Burgess's autobiography is an interesting book.
  d. Oscar Wilde was the author of *The Picture of Dorian Gray*.
  e. The last scene of the opera – when Mimi dies in front of her helpless friends – always brings tears to my eyes.
  f. *Venus and Adonis* is a famous poem by Shakespeare.
  g. The dialogue in Oscar Wilde's plays is always very good.
  h. Mickey Mouse is a very famous cartoon character.

6

3 | T.4.6.A. | | T.4.6.B. |

In the sentences, where *from*, *to*, *for*, *of*, and *at* come in the **middle**, the prepositions are unstressed and weak in pronunciation. In the questions, where *of*, *to*, *at*, *from*, and *for* come at the **end**, the prepositions are stressed and strong in pronunciation.

7

1 | T.4.7. |

   a. Can you tell me who wrote
      The French Lieutenant's
      Woman?
   b. Have you got any idea when
      it was written?
   c. Do you happen to know if
      The Magus has ever been
      made into a film?
   d. Do you know who the main
      characters in the book are?

2 The intonation falls at the end of
questions asked indirectly. This
falling pattern is always the
same.

8

1 | T.4.8.A. |

   a. . . . isn't he?
   b. . . . do you?
   c. . . . can it?
   d. . . . haven't you?
   e. . . . would you?
   f. . . . hasn't she?
   g. . . . was there?
   h. . . . did they?
   i. . . . wasn't it?
   j. . . . isn't she?
   k. . . . would you?
   l. . . . can't he?

2 a. R d. R g. R j. F
   b. F e. R h. F k. F
   c. F f. F i. R l. R

7 astrology = using the stars to
    predict the future
  phrenology = analysing people's
    character using the bumps on
    their heads
  claustrophobia = a fear of closed
    places
  entomology = the study of
    insects
  kleptomania = an unnatural
    desire to steal
  philately = stamp collecting
  agoraphobia = a fear of open
    spaces
  bibliophile = a book lover
  vertigo = a fear of high places
  ornithology = the study of birds

graphology = analysing people's
   character using their
   handwriting
etymology = the study of word
   origins

9

1 | T.4.9. |

   a. Aries   g. Taurus
   b. Pisces   h. Gemini
   c. Cancer   i. Capricorn
   d. Libra   j. Scorpio
   e. Leo   k. Aquarius
   f. Virgo   l. Sagittarius

UNIT 5

1

2 | T.5.1.B. |

   a. sin   d. thigh   g. tent
   b. tank   e. pass   h. face
   c. thick   f. taught i. fourth

2

2 | T.5.2.B. |

The / z / card is the first and the
/ ð / card is the second.

Zen
dare
breeze
clothing
loathe
ties
doze
lies
day
there
she's
southern
closing
tide
breathe
those
whizz
load
lied
den
she'd

they
lose
with
sudden
then
breed

3

2 | T.5.3. |

A How are Judith and Timothy
  Thorpe's triplets?
B Those three? Well . . . both
  Heather and Cathy are very
  healthy, but I think they're
  having rather a lot of trouble
  with Matthew.
A With Matthew? What's the
  matter with Matthew?
B Teething troubles, I think,
  and then he won't eat
  anything.
A Teething troubles? But how
  old are the triplets now?
B I think they're about thirteen
  months.
A Thirteen months? Oh, I
  thought they were a lot
  younger than that.
B No, they must be thirteen
  months because it was their
  first birthday at the end of last
  month – on the thirtieth . . .
  or was it the thirty-first?
A Oh dear, and I didn't send
  them anything, not even a
  birthday card . . . I wonder
  what Judith and Timothy
  thought?
B Don't distress yourself dear,
  they didn't say anything to
  me . . .

4

1 a. sun/son
   b. past/passed
   c. fair/fare
   d. bear/bare
   e. aloud/allowed
   f. sweet/suite

2   T.5.4.

a. Which channel is *My Fair Lady* on?
b. I don't know whether to go to the pool or not.
c. Whose watch is this on the floor?
d. He used to be a colonel in the army.
e. The dog wagged its tail happily.
f. A Is he one of the town councillors?
   B No, he's the mayor of the town.
g. I practise playing the guitar every day.
h. Most of the guerillas were armed with machine guns and hand grenades.
i. Brrr . . . Close the window! There's a terrible draught in here.
j. The lion gave a loud roar and then ran off.

5

1   T.5.5.

a. past	f. present
b. present	g. present
c. past	h. past
d. present	i. past
e. past	j. present

2   It is sometimes difficult to hear the difference between past and present tenses because the auxiliary verbs are either in their contracted form or else very weak. (e.g. I've, I'd, was / wəz /, were / wə /) Word linking can also make it difficult to hear any difference between present and past tenses.

Example

Present/Past

Who are you/who were you
He's sold/He sold
They've found/They found
like the/liked the
I've failed/I failed
wash the/washed the
She's cycled/She cycled
How are you/How were you

T.5.5.

a. Who were you waiting for?
b. He's sold the flat.
c. They found some money in the street.
d. We like the hotel.
e. They'd been waiting for ages.
f. I've failed my driving test.
g. She's enjoying her new job.
h. We washed the car on Sunday.
i. She cycled home.
j. How are you hoping to get there?

6

3   T.5.6.B.

In A the final *r* – normally silent in British English – is sounded, and links on to the next word: Mind your own business!
In B there is an extra sound / j / between the vowel sound at the end of the first word and the
                     / j /
vowel sound at the beginning of the next word: Pay attention!
In C there is an extra sound / w / between the vowel sound at the end of one word and the vowel sound at the beginning of the
                     / w /
next word: Here you are.

8

1   T.5.8.A.

a. Congratulations!
b. Bad luck!
c. Cheers!
d. Cheerio!
e. I'm sorry to hear that.
f. Good luck!
g. Have a good weekend!
h. Have a nice time!

3   T.5.8.B.

Suggested responses:

A I didn't pass my driving test.
B Bad luck!

A Another brandy?
B Cheers!

A Old Uncle Fred died last week.
B I'm sorry to hear that. (**not** 'Bad luck')

A I've got my job interview this afternoon.
B Good luck!

A Bye!
B Cheerio!

A I won't be here on Monday because we're off to Spain on holiday.
B Have a nice time!

A I passed all my exams.
B Congratulations!

A I'm just going to see the boss about my pay rise.
B Good luck!

9

4   T.5.9.

A   Airport

duty free shop

departure lounge

gate 12

passport control

check-in desk

baggage reclaim

B Railway station

● ● ●
ticket office

● ● ●
left luggage

● ● ●
waiting room

● ● ●
platform 10

C Both

● ● ●
arrivals board

● ● ●
departures board

● ● ●
taxi rank

● ● ● ●
lost property office

● ● ●
meeting point

● ● ●
information desk

10

| T.5.10.A. | You hear these clues on the tape.

a. At the end of the 15th century
b. In the first century BC
c. In the middle of the eighteenth century
d. At the beginning of the sixteenth century
e. In the fifth century BC
f. At the beginning of the eighteenth century
g. At the beginning of the nineteenth century
h. In the fourth century BC

1 a. 1492   e. 429 BC
   b. 44 BC   f. 1715
   c. 1762   g. 1804
   d. 1509   h. 323 BC

3 | T.5.10.B. |

M When did the French revolution start?
W In 1789, wasn't it?

M Ah, so it was at the end of the 18th century.
M When did Shakespeare die?
W In 1616, wasn't it?
M Ah, so it was at the beginning of the 17th century.
M When did Julius Caesar conquer Britain?
W In 55 BC, wasn't it?
M Ah, so it was in the 1st century BC.
M When did North America become independent?
W In 1776, wasn't it?
M Ah, so it was at the end of the 18th century.
M When did the modern Olympic Games start up?
W In 1896, wasn't it?
M Ah, so it was at the end of the 19th century.
M When did Queen Victoria die?
W In 1901, wasn't it?
M Ah, so it was at the beginning of the 20th century.
M When was Britain conquered by the Normans?
W In 1066, wasn't it?
M Ah, so it was in the middle of the 11th century.
M When was *The Communist Manifesto* published?
W In 1848, wasn't it?
M Ah, so it was in the middle of the 19th century.

UNIT 6

1

2 | T.6.1.C. |

Rob's list
chops
lobster
sausages
cauliflower
yoghurt
chocolate
coffee
oranges

Dawn's list
prawns
walnuts
courgettes
sweetcorn
strawberries

Joan's list
rolls
potatoes
cocoa
macaroni
avocados
coke
aubergines

2

1 | T.6.2. |

a. knee   g. knob
b. kneel   h. knock
c. knickers   i. knot
d. knife   j. know
e. knight   k. knowledge
f. knit   l. knuckle

3 When *k* comes before the letter *n* at the beginning of a word it is silent.

3

1 *Anti-* / æntɪ / as a prefix means *against*.

2 *Pro-* / prəʊ / as a prefix means *supporting* or *for*.

4 Some other common words with *anti-*:
antisocial   anti-clockwise
anti-climax   anti-depressant
anti-freeze   anti-semitic

4

1 | T.6.4.A. |

When the two are said together the *d* usually disappears from the end of *and*. This is called elision.

/ r /
In 'vodka and orange' there is an / r / sound linking the words 'vodka' and 'and'. This is called an intrusive r. Intrusive r links a word which ends in / ə / with the following word which begins with a vowel.

93

Other examples:

/ r /
vanilla ice cream

/ r /
a villa in Spain

/ r /
I've got no idea of the time.

3,4　T.6.4.B.

salt and pepper
cheese and biscuits
bread and butter
fish and chips
toast and marmalade
nuts and raisins
strawberries and cream
bacon and eggs
apple pie and custard

5

1　T.6.5.

a. **B** ■ He'd had a lot of drinks.

b. **B** She bought several ■ dresses.

c. **B** They lost everything ■ in the burglary.

d. **B** She's inherited a great deal ■ of money.

e. **B** Oh, he's been out with all ■ the girls in the village.

f. **B** Oh, they've spent all the ■ money they won.

g. **B** ■ Oh, everyone knows.

2　The words are stressed because Barbara is correcting a piece of information in what Alan said.

6

1　T.6.6.

The sentences with the following modal verbs are the ones that sound less polite.

a. shouldn't　　e. should
b. must　　　　f. oughtn't to
c. ought to　　g. ought to
d. mustn't

2　The intonation and stress pattern is more important in sounding polite than the modal verb you choose. Since *should* and *ought to* express *mild* obligation, it is especially important to be careful with intonation when using *must* for giving advice.

7

2　T.6.7.A.

a. Shall I call the doctor?
b. Could you get me some aspirin?
c. Shall I make you a nice cup of tea?
d. Shall I open the window a bit?
e. Would you buy me a magazine or something?
f. Do you think you could get this prescription for me?
g. Shall I give you a lift to the doctor's surgery?
h. Do you think you could phone the office for me?
i. Shall I pop in and see you tomorrow?

8

3　T.6.8.

A ● ●　　　B ● ● ●

fibre　　　vitamin
caffeine　calorie
protein　　saccharin
diet　　　 alcohol
　　　　　 mineral
　　　　　 additive
　　　　　 calcium

C ● ● ● ●　D ● ● ● ●

cholesterol　carbohydrate
preservative

9

T.6.9.

What does 15.15 mean?
Quarter past three.

What does 17.53 mean?
Seven minutes to six.

What does 19.35 mean?
Twenty-five to eight.

What does 13.03 mean?
Three minutes past one.

What does 22.45 mean?
Quarter to eleven.

What does 14.11 mean?
Eleven minutes past two.

What does 18.55 mean?
Five to seven.

What does 23.47 mean?
Thirteen minutes to midnight.

What does 16.12 mean?
Twelve minutes past four.

What does 21.40 mean?
Twenty to ten.

10

2　T.6.10.B.

What happened to inflation in 1984?
It fell to 8.5%.
What happened to government popularity in 1984?
It rose to 61%.
What happened to unemployment in 1984?
It fell to 5.5%.
What happened to government popularity in 1985?
It fell to 38%.
What happened to unemployment in 1986?
It rose to 10%.
What happened to inflation in 1986?
It fell to 21.9%.
What happened to inflation in 1987?
It rose to 28.2%.
What happened to unemployment in 1988?
It rose to 19.75%.
What happened to inflation in 1988?
It rose to 35%.
What happened to government popularity in 1988?
It fell to 28.5%.

UNIT 7

1

1 **T.7.1.A.**

   a. This code surprises me.
   b. I'm sure he's bald.
   c. We rolled over together.
   d. I need to be towed.
   e. It's an imaginary world.

2

1 **T.7.2.A.**

1

/ ɑ: /	/ ɔ: /	/ ʊ /
half	chalk	should
calm	talk	could
calf	walk	would
almond	stalk	
palm		
behalf		

/ əʊ /	/ æ /
yolk	salmon
folk	

3 The letters *olk* are pronounced
/ əʊk /.
The letters *alk* are pronounced
/ ɔ:k /.
The letters *ould* are pronounced
/ ʊd /.
The letters *alf* are pronounced
/ ɑ: f /.
The letters *alm* are pronounced
/ ɑ: m / or / æm /.

5   walkman   talkative
     walking stick   palmistry, etc.

3

1 **T.7.3.A.**

/ tʃ /	/ k /
chip	chemical
bachelor	masochist
children	Christian
rich	mechanic
chance	character
choice	cholera

champion   technology
macho   psychiatric
research   choir
parched   echo

4 **T.7.3.B.**

In *yacht* the *ch* is silent.
In *machine*, *sachet*, *chef*,
chauffeur, *champagne*, *brochure*,
and *moustache* it is pronounced
/ ʃ /.

4

1 **T.7.4.A.**

   a. Which subject did you hate
      most at school?

   b. Just give him a minute
      amount of this medicine.

   c. She got a prize for good
      conduct at school this term.

   d. Who's going to minute this
      meeting?

   e. He's a British subject, isn't
      he?

   f. I won't be a minute, darling.

   g. They're going to conduct an
      enquiry into the problem.

   h. I won't subject you to any
      more questions.

2 a. / raʊ /   g. / kləʊz /
   b. / rəʊ /   h. / kləʊs /
   c. / bəʊ /   i. / tɪə /
   d. / baʊ /   j. / teə /
   e. / wɪnd /   k. / laɪv /
   f. / waɪnd /   l. / lɪv /

5

1

Subject	Person
ecology	ecologist
psychology	psychologist
biology	biologist
astrology	astrologer
archaeology	archaeologist
sociology	sociologist
geology	geologist
zoology	zoologist
theology	theologian

Adjective	
ecological	sociological
psychological	geological
biological	zoological
astrological	theological
archaeological	

2 **T.7.5.**

ecology   sociology
ecologist   sociologist
ecological   sociological

psychology   geology
psychologist   geologist
psychological   geological

biology   zoology
biologist   zoologist
biological   zoological

astrology   theology
astrologer   theologian
astrological   theological

archaeology
archaeologist
archaeological

6

1 T.7.6.

● ● ● ●   ● ● ●

feminism   fascism
optimism   Buddhism
socialism   sexism
communism
cynicism
fatalism   ● ● ● ● ●
pessimism
realism   Catholicism
chauvinism   consumerism
heroism   materialism

                ● ● ● ●

                capitalism

3 a. feminists
   b. chauvinists
   c. Catholics
   d. Buddhists
   e. cynics
   f. heroes . . . heroines

7

2 white gloves / k /
   red carpet / g /
   green card / ŋ /
   red pepper / b /
   brown paper / m /
   white bread / p / .
   gold medal / b /
   white coffee / k /
   brown belt / m /
   green goddess / ŋ /
   red gold / g /
   Green Movement / m /
   white magic / p /
   red-brick / b /
   white paper / p /

4 / t / changes to / k / in front of / k /
   and / g / and to / p / in front of
   / p /, / m /, and / b /.
   / d / changes to / g / in front of
   / k / and / g / and to / b / in front
   of / p /, / m /, and / b /.
   / n / changes to / ŋ / in front of / k /
   and / g / and to / m / in front of
   / p /, / m /, and / b /.

8

4 T.7.8.C.

I really have no idea exactly
what I'll be doing – or even
where I'll be – in the year 2000.
Of course I'll be 43 years old;
and I expect I'll have a wife and
children by then. It's funny, but I
sometimes find myself thinking
of New Year's Eve on the 31st of
December 1999. It's going to be
rather exciting: listening to the
radio, waiting for Big Ben to
bring in the new year, the new
century, and the new
millennium.

   People are always afraid of the
future because it's unknown; but
I have a feeling that historians in
the mid 21st century may well
look back on the ups and downs
of the late 20th century and say
to themselves: 'Well, things
might have been worse!'.

9

3 T.7.9.A.

Sentences a and c are unlikely
possibilities. The stress and
intonation pattern in these
sentences is like this:

She might come tomorrow.

He may come later.

The stress and intonation pattern
in the other sentences is like this:

She might come tomorrow.

He may come later.

5 a. u   d. –   g. –   j. –
   b. u   e. –   h. –   k. –
   c. –   f. u   i. u   l. u

10

1 T.7.10.A.

nine
ninety-nine
nine hundred and ninety-nine
nine thousand, nine hundred,
   and ninety-nine
ninety-nine thousand, nine
   hundred, and ninety-nine
nine hundred and ninety-nine
   thousand, nine hundred, and
   ninety-nine
nine million, nine hundred and
   ninety-nine thousand, nine
   hundred, and ninety-nine

2 T.7.10.B.

Beijing	9,230,000
Bombay	5,970,575
Budapest	2,058,000
Cairo	8,500,000
London	7,028,200
Madrid	3,792,561
Moscow	6,941,961
Munich	1,314,865
New York	7,035,000
Paris	2,168,300
Rome	2,897,819
Saõ Paulo	8,732,000
Sydney	3,021,299
Tokyo	8,448,382

4

Mexico City	31,000,000
Saõ Paolo	25,800,000
Tokyo	24,200,000
New York	22,800,000
Shanghai	22,700,000
Beijing	19,900,000
Rio de Janeiro	19,000,000
Bombay	17,000,000
Calcutta	16,700,000
Jakarta	16,600,000

(Figures based on UN estimates
and projections.)

UNIT 8

1

2 [T.8.1.B.]

shoots
seats
saves
sea
Sue
shy
sign
sock
sore
short
so
sewn
shield
fist
said
shell
sack
rust
suits
shown
she

Card A gets the first row of crosses
(so, seats, shell, shy)
Card C gets the most rows – three
(sock, saves, shown, fist)
(she, saves, short, so)
(sack, fist, suits, shy)
Card B gets two rows
(Sue, suits, sea, sack)
(sore, shown, Sue, rust)
Card A also gets another row
(Sue, rust, short, fist)

6 Sample story:
Last summer, before she went to
the Spanish sea shore disco,
Shirley shaved her legs, because
she said the hairs showed. Soon
after, Sean Stewart saw her
standing outside the disco
wearing plastic shoes,
sunglasses, and sexy shorts. He
smiled.

2

1 a. cigars   g. pyjamas
  b. rocks   h. figs
  c. fools   i. matches
  d. grapes   j. features
  e. cheeses   k. reflections
  f. garments l. confidences

2 a. / z / e.g. cigars/pyjamas/
    features.
  b. / z / e.g. fools/figs/reflections.
  c. / s / e.g. rocks/grapes/
    garments.
  d. / ɪz / e.g. cheeses/matches/
    confidences.

4 [T.8.2.B.]

The rules are the **same** with the
third person singular *s*
and *'s*.

5 [T.8.2.C.]

Before a consonant (except *h*) *s*
is always pronounced / s / and
never / z /.

3

2 [T.8.3.]

A	B
industry	castle
eastern	Christmas
often	listen
faster	whistle
gangster	often
youngster	fasten
	mortgage
	soften
	rustle
	wrestler

(*often* can go in both columns)

3 a. The letters *-stle* at the end of a
    word are pronounced / sl /.
  b. The letters *-sten* at the end of
    a word are pronounced / sn /.

4

1 well-dressed
  well-behaved
  self-centred
  broad-shouldered
  narrow-minded

3 [T.8.4.A.]

self-confident
self-conscious
badly-dressed
badly-behaved
over-confident
overweight
over-dressed
narrow-shouldered
broad-minded

6 [T.8.4.B.]

a. She's always so well-dressed.

b. They're well-behaved
   children really.

c. He's so narrow-minded, isn't
   he?

d. Are you left-handed,
   Margery?

e. The police are looking for a

   clean-shaven youth who was
   spotted at the scene of the
   crime.

f. Sharon's got a really good-
   looking boyfriend.

g. Don't be so self-centred!

h. It's difficult working for a

   bad-tempered boss.

i. I'm not going to marry an

   overweight businessman!

The main stress is on the first
word when the compound
adjectives are followed by a
noun. In other cases the main
stress is on the second word.

5

1 [T.8.5.]

  a. 6   e. 8
  b. 8   f. 16
  c. 10   g. 10
  d. 10   h. 9

2   a. Can I get past you, please?
    b. Get me a pair of scissors, will you?
    c. So what time did you get back from the party?
    d. Sorry, I just couldn't get away from the office.
    e. Unfortunately we couldn't get into the stadium.
    f. Get in touch with me as soon as you get to the airport, won't you?
    g. I shouldn't think I'll get in before midnight.
    h. I'll get you something to drink, shall I?

4   a. Can I pass by you, please?
    b. Fetch me a pair of scissors, will you?
    c. So what time did you return from the party?
    d. Sorry, I just couldn't leave the office.
    e. Unfortunately, we couldn't enter the stadium.
    f. Contact me as soon as you reach the airport, won't you?
    g. I shouldn't think I'll arrive home before midnight.
    h. I'll fetch you something to drink, shall I?

6

1   filthy   clean
    ugly   attractive
    boring   exciting
    childish   mature
    messy   tidy
    unfriendly   sociable
    narrow-minded   tolerant
    badly-behaved   well-behaved
    impractical   practical
    bad-tempered   patient
    deceitful   honest

3   T.8.6.A.

    a. clean
    b. tidy
    c. attractive
    d. tasteful

B is more tactful, because:
– she uses the *not very* + positive adjective form.
– the hesitation makes her sound more tactful.
– she doesn't use such emphatic intonation as A.

6   T.8.6.B.

A   The parents are so unfriendly!
B   Mmm . . . they aren't very sociable, are they?
A   And they're so narrow-minded!
B   Mmm . . . they're not very tolerant, are they?
A   And the children are so badly-behaved!
B   Mmm . . . they aren't very well-behaved, are they?
A   David is so boring!
B   Mmm . . . he's not very exciting, is he?
A   And he's so bad-tempered!
B   Mmm . . . he's not very patient, is he?
A   Janet's so childish!
B   Mmm . . . she's not very mature, is she?
A   And she's so deceitful!
B   Mmm . . . she's not very honest, is she?
A   And the whole family are so impractical!
B   Mmm . . . they're not very practical, are they?

7

2   T.8.7.A.

A   . . . so he was a short man?

B   No, he was a tall man.
A   . . . and fair-haired, you said?

B   No, dark-haired.
A   . . . and he was in his mid-forties . . .?

B   In his mid-thirties.
A   And you said he was wearing an expensive-looking grey suit . . .

B   I said he was wearing an expensive-looking white suit.
A   And he was carrying a knife, wasn't he?

B   No, he was carrying a gun.
A   And you saw him going into the post office?

B   No, I saw him going out of the post office.
A   And he got away with five thousand pounds . . .

B   No, he got away with ten thousand pounds.
A   Well, thank you very much for your help.
B   Not at all.

    a. short   e. knife
    b. fair   f. into
    c. forties   g. five
    d. grey

3   a. tall   e. gun
    b. dark   f. out
    c. thirties   g. ten
    d. white

These words are stressed because B wants to correct the mistakes that A makes.

6   T.8.7.B.

A   . . . so the woman was sixty-five years old . . .?

B   No, she was seventy-five years old.
A   . . . and she was carrying a handbag and a purse.
B   No, she was carrying a shopping bag and a purse.
A   And she only had three pounds fifty with her, you say?

B   No, she only had one pound fifty with her.
A   And there were four youths, weren't there?

B   No, there were three youths.
A   . . . who were wearing denim jackets . . .

B No, they were wearing leather jackets.

A And they were carrying guns?

B No, they were carrying ■ knives.

8

1,2 T.8.8.A.

a. **A** I'm absolutely *exhausted*, aren't you?
   B Well . . . I'm quite *tired*.

b. **A** I thought the meal was absolutely *delicious*, didn't you?
   B Well . . . it was quite *tasty*.

c. **A** I'm absolutely *starving*, aren't you?
   B Well . . . I'm quite *hungry*.

d. **A** I thought the scenery was absolutely *beautiful*, didn't you?
   B Well . . . it was quite *pretty*.

The first speaker shows the strongest feelings by:
– choosing a very strong adjective
– using an extreme modifier (see page 74 of the Student's Book)
– his intonation which is very emphatic (high fall).

The second speaker shows that she has mixed feelings by:
– choosing a less strong adjective
– using 'quite' as a modifier
– her intonation which shows reservations (fall-rise).

9

2 T.8.9.A.

a. triangle   triangular

b. curve   curved

c. rectangle   rectangular

d. cylinder   cylindrical

e. square   square

f. hexagon   hexagonal

g. oval   oval

h. circle   circular/round

i. semi-circle   semi-circular

j. cube   cubic/cube-shaped

k. sphere   spherical

l. octagon   octagonal

5 T.8.9.B.

You're going to draw a robot. The robot has a cylindrical body . . . and a cube-shaped head . . . Both of his legs are long thin cylinders . . . His arms are rectangular, but long and thin too. . . His hands are small and triangular . . . and his feet small and square . . . Both of his eyes are hexagonal . . . and he has a large semi-circular mouth – smiling . . . and a small round nose . . . On the front of his body there is a large octagon.

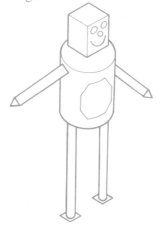

UNIT 9

1

1 T.9.1.A.

a. 1 van   2 ban
b. 1 vest   2 best
c. 1 bars   2 vase

d. 1 votes   2 boats
e. 1 bet   2 vet
f. 1 berry   2 very
g. 1 fibre   2 fiver
h. 1 dove   2 dub

2

1 lamb climb bombardment thumb combination numb bomb dumb comb number crumb debt limb doubt crumble plumber limbo subtle subtitle lumber

4 When the letters *mb* or *bt* come at the end of a word, *b* is silent. Some other words like *subtle* and *plumber*, for example, also contain silent *b*.

3

3 T.9.3.

A / e /	B / ɪə /
health	theatre
leather	appeared
death	ideal

C / iː /	D / ɜː /
feature	earn
pleased	heard
leave	rehearsing
teacher	
increases	
colleagues	

E / eɪ /	F / eə /
break	wears
	yeah

4 The most common pronunciation of *ea* is / i: /. Here are some more words spelt with *ea*:

A / e /	B / ɪə /
bread	beard
breath	clear
dead	dear
head	ear
heavy	fear
instead	gear
measure	hear
pleasure	near
ready	realistic
sweat	realize
thread	year
tread	
treasure	
wealthy	
weather	

C / i: /	D / ɜ: /
beach	earl
bead	heard
bean	learn
beat	pearl
breathe	research
clean	
each	
easy	**E / eɪ /**
heal	
heat	great
meal	steak
mean	
meat	**F / eə /**
neat	
peach	bear
reach	pear
reading	swear
reason	
seat	
speak	
steal	
stream	
weak	

4

2 T.9.4.A.

a. granddaughter
b. great-grandmother
c. ex-husband
d. stepmother
e. half-sister
f. great-nephew
g. second cousin
h. mother-in-law
i. ex-boyfriend
j. son-in-law

4 T.9.4.B.

a. Who is my wife's father?
b. Who is my aunt's daughter?
c. Who are my mother's mother's parents?
d. Who is my nephew's daughter?
e. Who is my husband's brother's wife?
f. Who is my father and step-mother's son?
g. Who is my mother's new husband's daughter by his first marriage?
h. Who is my father's cousin?

a. my father-in-law
b. my cousin
c. my great-grandparents
d. my great-niece
e. my sister-in-law
f. my half-brother
g. my step-sister
h. my second cousin

5

5 The correct words are:

a. raise
b. breath
c. use / ju: s /
d. rise
e. breathe
f. bath
g. use / ju: z /
h. bathe

6

3 T.9.6.

a. We're as different as chalk and cheese.
b. Patrick and Jenny get on like a house on fire.
c. It was love at first sight.
   / m /
d. She really gets on my nerves.
e. They're head over heels in love.
f. We're not on speaking terms any more.
   / j / /w // j /
g. They don't see eye to eye on anything.

7

1 T.9.7.A.

a. A Is it snowing outside?
   B No, it can't be snowing – it's too early in the year for snow.

b. A Is that new snack bar round the corner good?
   B It must be good – everyone in the office goes there for lunch.

c. A Has Bill gone home already?
   B No, he can't have gone home – his briefcase's still here.

d. A Have you met Simon before?
   B I must have met him before – he seemed to recognise me.

2 *Have* is pronounced / əv /:
can't have / kɑ:ntəv /
must have / mʌstəv /.
Be is pronounced / bɪ /:
can't be / kɑ:mpbɪ /
must be / mʌsbɪ /.

3 [T.9.7.B.]
a. A Are the children sleeping?
   B They must be sleeping – everything's so quiet.
b. A Is Sue still ill?
   B She can't be ill – she's gone to work.
c. A Has Carol been on a diet?
   B She must have been on a diet – she looks a lot slimmer.
d. A Is Hannah still studying?
   B She can't be studying – all the lights are off.
e. A Have Anna and Pete split up?
   B They must have split up – she's got a new boyfriend.
f. A Has David got financial problems?
   B He can't have financial problems – he's just bought a new car.
g. A Do Jeff and Linda get on well?
   B They must get on well – they're always together.
h. A Have the neighbours gone on holiday yet?
   B They can't have gone on holiday – I saw them in the garden this morning.
i. A Is Gillian speaking to her boyfriend?
   B She must be speaking to her boyfriend – she's been on the phone for hours.
j. A Is Elaine's husband American?
   B He can't be American – he sounds so British.

9

4

[T.9.9.D.]

5 Suggestions as to why the intonation might sound surprised.
   b. For some reason Jason is a strange person to ask.
   c. £2,000 is a lot of money to lend – or perhaps Rob is not usually so generous.
   f. This is a ridiculous complaint.

10

1 [T.9.10.A.]
a. She took off her hat.
b. She took her hat off.
c. She took it off.

2 [T.9.10.B.]
A They're going to pull down the old school.
B The old school?
A Yes. They're going to pull it down.
A Can't you give up smoking?
B Smoking?
A Yes. Can't you give it up?
A You haven't phoned up Auntie Freda.
B Auntie Freda?
A Yes. You haven't phoned her up.
A Ronald's shaved off his moustache.
B His moustache?
A Yes. He's shaved it off.
A I threw away your old football socks.
B My old football socks?
A Yes. I threw them away.
A Have you written down my measurements?
B Your measurements?
A Yes. Have you written them down?

A He nearly cut his finger off.
B His finger?
A Yes. He nearly cut it off.
A Turn off the lights, will you?
B The lights?
A Yes. Turn them off, will you?
A She picked up the broken vase.
B The broken vase?
A Yes. She picked it up.
A They've turned down the latest pay offer.
B The latest pay offer?
A Yes. They've turned it down.
A She put on her sunglasses.
B Her sunglasses?
A Yes. She put them on.
A Put away that magazine.
B This magazine?
A Yes. Put it away.

11

2 [T.9.11]

A	B
Prime Minister	Queen
General Secretary	Emperor
Chairman	Lord
Ambassador	Lady
Consul	Prince
Vice-President	Sheikh
President	Countess
Chancellor	Duke
	Empress
	Shah
	Princess
	Count
	Duchess
	King

C	D
Cardinal	General
Archbishop	Sergeant
Bishop	Colonel
Rabbi	Admiral
Pope	Captain
Vicar	Lieutenant

```
G E N E R A L S E C R E T A R Y
Q U E E N M E M P E R O R C D V
A S C L B B C H A I R M A N D I
P E A O R A R C H B I S H O P C
R R R R A S M O P R I N C E O A
I G D D B S O L S H E I K H P R
M E I L B A C O U N T E S S E G
E A N A I D P N D C O N S U L U
M N A D J O N E U E M P R E S S
I T L Y R R Q L K L K S H A H I
N V I C E P R E S I D E N T J
I P R I N C E S S C O U N T U V
S S C C H A N C E L L O R W X Y
T A D E B D U C H E S S K I N G
E A D M I R A L C A P T A I N Z
R L L I E U T E N A N T F K R Z
```

UNIT 10

1

2 **T.10.1.**

1. psychologist
2. pterodactyl
3. pneumonia
4. pseudonym
5. pneumatic
6. psychiatrist
7. cupboard
8. receipt
9. psychic
10. psalm

3 The initial letter *p* is silent in words that begin with *ps*, *pt*, and *pn*. Some other words like *cupboard* and *receipt*, for example, also contain silent *p*.

2

1

/ f /	silent *gh*	/ g /
rough	plough	ghost
laughter	through	ghastly
cough	slaughter	gherkin
tough	drought	ghoulish

6 When the letters *gh* come at the beginning of a word they are always pronounced / g /.

3

1,2 **T.10.3.A.**

/ ʌ /	/ ʊ /
puzzle	pudding
lucky	bush
pub	bullet

/ u: /	/ ju: /
rude	unite
flute	utensil
conclusion	amused

5
a. cheque   f. guest
b. vague   g. guarantee
c. guard   h. queue
d. quiet   i. banquet
e. quite   j. bouquet

4

1 *Interested* is the word that changes meaning with *un-* and *dis-*. Check *uninterested* and *disinterested* in a dictionary if you are not sure of the difference.

2 **T.10.4.**

un-	unreasonable
untidy	unacceptable
unadventurous	*dis-*
unsatisfied	dissatisfied
uncomfortable	dishonest
unreliable	disagreeable
unsociable	disinterested
uninterested	disloyal

3

• • ●	• ● • •
untidy	unsatisfied
dishonest	uncomfortable
disloyal	unsociable
	uninterested
	unreasonable
• • ● • •	dissatisfied
	disinterested
unadventurous	
unreliable	
disagreeable	
unacceptable	

5

1 a. She's as blind as a bat.
   b. He's as stubborn as a mule.
   c. She's as strong as an ox.
   d. He's as proud as a peacock.
   e. He drinks like a fish.
   f. She eats like a pig.

3 a. a chimney   e. gold
   b. a trooper   f. sin
   c. a hatter   g. lead
   d. a fiddle   h. a log

6

2 **T.10.6.A.**

I usually drink tea. It's better than the coffee here.
I can't get used to the British weather. It's so changeable.
I'm used to driving on the right, not the left.
I used to think double-decker buses were very strange before I came to London.

5 **T.10.6.B.**

a. No, but she used to.
b. Because they're used to it.
c. No, but there used to be.
d. Yes, but I'm slowly getting used to it.
e. No, I expect she's used to them.
f. They're used to it.
g. No, but I used to.
h. Yes, but I soon got used to it.

7 **T.10.6.C.**

a. . . . get up?
b. . . . spend Christmas?
c. . . . do on Sunday morning?
d. . . . go to for advice?
e. . . . have for breakfast?
f. . . . go to bed?
g. . . . do on Saturday evening?
h. . . . spend New Year's Eve?

7

1 In the phrases on the right, the tongue moves into position to make the first plosive, but the sound is not pronounced. Instead there is a short, silent hesitation.

3 `T.10.7.B.`

  a. She was wearing a deep purple evening dress.
  b. They had dinner at nine o'clock.
  c. We've got a flat tyre, I'm afraid.
  d. She gave him a quick kiss.
  e. You're a big girl now, dear.
  f. He didn't do the washing-up.
  g. We had a really good time at Antonia's.
  h. What are my job prospects after the course?
  i. Mmm! I love ripe bananas!
  j. Give that ball a big kick!
  k. They've got a lovely back garden.

8

1 b. cowardly
  c. humble
  d. attractive
  e. spoilt
  f. generous
  g. modest
  h. hard-working
  i. sophisticated

2 `T.10.8.A.`

  a. Arthur's taciturn?
  b. Jane's brave?
  c. Julian's proud?
  d. Andrea's plain.
  e. Amanda's well-brought-up?
  f. Paul's tight-fisted.
  g. Sally's big-headed.
  h. Peter's lazy?
  i. Mary's naive?

4 `T.10.8.B.`

  A Arthur's so taciturn!
  B Arthur's taciturn? I thought he was rather talkative myself.

  A Sally's awfully big-headed!
  B Sally's big-headed? I thought she was rather modest myself.
  A Julian's terribly proud!
  B Julian's proud? I thought he was rather humble myself.
  A Mary's really naive!
  B Mary's naive? I thought she was rather sophisticated myself.
  A Amanda's really well-brought-up!
  B Amanda's well-brought-up? I thought she was rather spoilt myself.
  A Jane's awfully brave!
  B Jane's brave? I thought she was rather cowardly myself.
  A Peter's terribly lazy!
  B Peter's lazy? I thought he was rather hard-working myself.
  A Andrea's very plain!
  B Andrea's plain? I thought she was rather attractive myself.
  A Paul's so tight-fisted!
  B Paul's tight-fisted? I thought he was rather generous myself.

9

2 a. I'd rather have my tea with lemon actually.
  b. During the school holidays we'd work in the pub.
  c. You'd better take a taxi, darling.
  d. You'd already left the airport by then.
  e. He said he'd come and join us after the opera.
  f. From time to time she'd buy me expensive presents.
  g. You'd be better off going straight to bed, my dear.
  h. She told me she'd got another job.
  i. I'd hate to be married to a miser.
  j. He'd never lived on a desert island before.

10

1 Australian dollar
  Austrian schilling
  Danish kroner
  Dutch guilder
  French franc
  German mark
  Greek drachma
  Italian lira
  Japanese yen
  Portuguese escudo
  Spanish peseta
  Yugoslav dinar

2 `T.10.10.`

  £1 buys:
  4,800 Yugoslav dinars
  2.095 Australian dollars
  248 Greek drachmas
  253 Portuguese escudos
  10.48 French francs
  3.48 Dutch guilders
  11.87 Danish kroner
  2,300 Italian lire
  3.08 German marks
  203.5 Spanish pesetas
  21.65 Austrian schillings
  223.5 Japanese yen

3 a. £13   d. £150
  b. £32   e. £20
  c. £15   f. £75

4 zloty – Poland
  rouble – USSR
  forint – Hungary
  shekel – Israel

UNIT 11

1

1 `T.11.1.A.`

  a. Are you choking?
  b. I got another batch yesterday.
  c. Listen to those cheers!
  d. They started surging upstairs.
  e. What a big gin you've got!

4 T.11.1.C.

/ dʒ /	/ tʃ /
original	teacher
unabridged	touch
teenager	eventually
energies	lecturer
judgement	achieve
savage	lunch
suggested	
disadvantage	
enjoyed	
intelligent	
just	
general	
largely	

2

1,2 T.11.2.A.

/ s /	/ z /
insult	please
goose	result
increase	lose
dose	vase
chase	choose

/ ʃ /	/ ʒ /
surely	leisure
ensure	usually
sure	pleasure
sugar	treasure
insurance	casual

3 a. permissive / s / (not / ʃ /)
   b. conclusion / ʒ / (not / ʃ /)
   c. assume / s / (not / ʃ /)
   d. dishevelled / ʃ / (not / s /)

3

1 In the word *shepherd* the letters *ph* are not pronounced as / f /. They are pronounced / p /. This and *shepherdess* are exceptions to the general rule.

4

2 T.11.4.

  a. no overtaking
  b. no u-turns
  c. no motor vehicles
  d. pedestrian crossing
  e. traffic lights
  f. end of dual carriageway
  g. road-works
  h. roundabout
  i. crossroads
  j. no entry
  k. no through road
  l. cyclists only
  m. hump bridge
  n. slippery road
  o. quayside or river bank

4 a. quayside   e. dual
   b. cyclists   f. carriageway
   c. traffic   g. pedestrian
   d. vehicles

5

1. T.11.5.

  1. a. She got a lovely present from her aunt, who lives in Canada.
     b. She got a lovely present from her aunt who lives in Canada.
  2. a. 'The taxi driver', said the cyclist, 'was the cause of the accident'.
     b. The taxi driver said the cyclist was the cause of the accident.
  3. a. The cassette recorder, which we bought last year, was stolen.
     b. The cassette recorder which we bought last year was stolen.
  4. a. Please don't come here again for my sake.
     b. Please don't come here again, for my sake.
  5. a. The workers, who asked for a pay rise, were sacked.
     b. The workers who asked for a pay rise were sacked.

2 1. a. Her only aunt sent her a present. This woman lives in Canada.
     b. She has more than one aunt. The Canadian aunt sent the present.
  2. a. The cyclist said it was the taxi driver's fault.
     b. The taxi driver said it was the cyclist's fault.
  3. a. Our one cassette recorder was stolen. We bought it last year.
     b. One of our cassette recorders was stolen. The one we bought last year.
  4. a. Come here if you want, but not because of me.
     b. If my well-being is important to you, don't come here.
  5. a. All the workers asked for a pay rise. All were sacked.
     b. Some of the workers asked for a pay rise. Those people were sacked.

6

1 a. 12 c. 14 e. 12 g. 13
   b. 13 d. 12 f. 11 h. 15

2 T.11.6.

  a. He might not have skidded if the road hadn't been icy.
  b. If we'd been going much faster, we might all have been killed.
  c. We couldn't have afforded it if she hadn't taken her credit card.
  d. If they'd searched more carefully, they might have found the jewels.
  e. Things would have been perfect if the engine hadn't caught fire.
  f. If she'd gone by plane, it would have been simpler.
  g. We wouldn't have crashed into him if he hadn't braked suddenly.
  h. If I'd known what was going to happen, I probably wouldn't have gone.

3 would have / ˈwʊdəv /
wouldn't have / ˈwʊdəntəv /

might have / ˈmaɪtəv /

might not have / ˈmaɪt nɒtəv /

could have / ˈkʊdəv /

couldn't have / ˈkʊdəntəv /

4 Sample story:
If I'd known what was going to happen, I probably wouldn't have gone. But I didn't know . . . and I went.
Just outside Vienna we hit some ice on the road, skidded, and crashed into the car in front. Well, maybe we wouldn't have crashed into him if he hadn't braked suddenly.
Frank, our driver, was really angry with himself. Of course he might not have skidded if the road hadn't been icy. Anyway, thanks to Frank we reached Vienna but if we'd been going much faster, we might all have been killed.

7

2 T.11.7.A.

a. have you? f. did it?
b. were you? g. has she?
c. did you? h. are you?
d. was she? i. am I?
e. did she? j. do you?

T.11.7.B.

4 A You know me.
B Oh, I do, do I?

A You've read my books.
B Oh, I have, have I?

A I was born in Belfast.
B Oh, you were, were you?

A I left school at 15.
B Oh, you did, did you?

A School's a waste of time.
B Oh, it is, is it?

A I'm a millionaire.
B Oh, you are, are you?

A I live in Jersey.
B Oh, you do, do you?

A I've got four marvellous kids.
B Oh, you have, have you?

A My latest book will be out in October.
B Oh, it will, will it?
A Life has been a disappointment.
B Oh, it has, has it?

8

2 T.11.8.A.

a. Do come in!
b. I do hope she gets better soon!
c. I have missed you!
d. You did promise!
e. I would be grateful!
f. I am sorry!
g. Do help yourself!
h. I did warn her!
i. He will be pleased!
j. Do hurry up!

5 T.11.8.B.

a. A Oh, I would be grateful!
b. C Oh, I am sorry!
c. E Oh, Frank, you did promise!
d. G Helen, do hurry up!
e. J There's some more left if you're still feeling hungry. Do help yourself!
f. L My Eric! Has he really? Oh, he will be pleased!

9

1 b. Acquired Immune Deficiency Syndrome
c. British Broadcasting Corporation
d. Before Christ
e. European Community
f. Intelligence Quotient
g. United Kingdom
h. Member of the British Empire
i. Ministry of Transport
j. Member of Parliament
k. Union of European Football Associations
l. Prime Minister
m. Royal Air Force
n. United Nations
o. United States
p. Union of Soviet Socialist Republics
q. Value Added Tax

4 T.11.9.B.

The abbreviations occur in this order:
MP
MBE
UEFA
UK
MOT
EC
US
AIDS
USSR
BC
AD

UNIT 12

1

1 T.12.1.A.

a. Is this a new pen?
b. The men from the council came today.
c. She's sad to be leaving.
d. What's the celery like?
e. I don't like landing, you know.

4

	1	2	3	4
A	man	men	band	ten
B	landing	tan	flesh	pan
C	flesh	celery	pan	men
D	men	lending	pen	salary

T.12.1.C.

A Right. What's in A1?
B A1? . . . *man*.
A And A2?
B A2 is *men*.
A And what about B1?
B B1 . . . *landing*.
A And C1?
B C1? . . . *flesh*.
A Aha! And B2?
B *Tan*.
A OK. And what about A3?
B A3 is *band*.
A And A4?
B A4 is *ten*.
A Right. And B3?

B B3 ... er ... *flesh*.
A Aha! Now what's in C2?
B C2 is *celery*.
A And D1? What's in that?
B D1 is *men*.
A Hmm. And D2?
B D2 ... *lending*.
A C3?
B C3 is ... wait a minute ... *pan*.
A OK. And B4?
B B4 is *pan*.
A I see. Now what about C4?
B C4 is *men*.
A And D3?
B D3 is *pen*.
A And, last but not least, what's in D4?
B D4 – last but not least – is *salary*.

2

2 T.12.2.A.

a. rhyme   climb
b. half   laugh
c. write   knight
d. sword   gnawed
e. knee   quay
f. wreck   cheque
g. limb   hymn
h. know   though
i. who   through
j. plant   aunt
k. rustle   muscle
l. funny   money
m. farm   psalm
n. bet   debt
o. smile   aisle
p. diet   quiet

5 T.12.2.B.

a. gnawed ... sword.
b. aunt ... plant.
c. cheque ... wreck.
d. debt ... bet.
e. smile ... aisle.
f. know ... though.
g. limb ... hymn.
h. through ... who.

3

1 a. handkerchief   l. leopard
  b. muscle   m. Thames
  c. aisle   n. autumn
  d. condemn   o. buoy
  e. Wednesday   p. corps
  f. biscuit   q. solemn
  g. phlegm   r. Leicester
  h. island   s. handsome
  i. sandwich   t. ironing
  j. hymn   u. bruise
  k. circuit

3 T.12.3.B.

A Do have a biscuit.
B A biscuit?
A See you on Wednesday.
B On Wednesday?
A I think I've strained a muscle.
B A muscle?
A I really love the Thames.
B The Thames?
A She's got a pet leopard.
B A pet leopard?
A He lives on a desert island.
B On a desert island?
A Have you been to Leicester?
B To Leicester?
A I hate doing the ironing.
B The ironing?

4

2 T.12.4.

a. break-in   f. fall-out
   break in   fall out
b. lookout   g. takeoff
   look out   take off
c. breakdown   h. send-off
   break down   send off
d. make-up   i. sell-out
   make up   sell out
e. drop-out   j. comeback
   drop out   come back

3 The stress in multi-word nouns is always on the first part:

●   ●   ●

look-out, breakdown, make-up, etc.

The stress in multi-word verbs varies. The usual pattern is

● ●, but sometimes it can be
● ●, depending on the context.

Example

● ●

Look out, Fred!

The stress in all the multi-word verbs in this exercise is regular:

● ●

break in, look out, etc.

5

1 T.12.5.A.

2, 3, 5, 8, 10, 11, 14, 16

3 a. 1   e. 8   i. 9   m. 6
  b. 5   f. 7   j. 2   n. 16
  c. 12 g. 11 k. 3   o. 14
  d. 4   h. 13 l. 10 p. 15

1 T.12.6.

/ j /   / j /
Today is the first day of the
                         / j /
rest of your life ... enjoy it!
/ g /
Lord give me patience –
/ p /   / k /
but make it quick!
Due to lack of interest
                  / ŋ /
tomorrow has been cancelled.
                  / j /
A Is there any intelligent life on earth?
B Yes, but I'm only visiting.
                  / j /
I used to be indecisive, but
/ w /
now I'm not so sure.
         / j / / k /
Feel strongly about graffiti?
Sign a partition.

A Why do people always
    / m /
write on blank walls?
B Because typing on them
    / b /
would be hard.
A In the beginning
  / g /   / b /
God created man.
B Yes, but She was
  / p /   / m /
just practising. And
practice after all
makes perfect.
             / m /
Nationalize crime and make
        / mp /
sure it doesn't pay.

7

2   **T.12.7.A.**

disgusting	delicious
cruel	kind
ugly	attractive
sensible	foolish
stale	fresh
cheap	expensive
warm	cold
smart	shabby
lovely	horrible
cheerful	depressing
important	insignificant
varied	monotonous

4

General	Particular
food	meal
clothes	dress
advice	suggestion
bread	loaf
luggage	case
rubbish	mess
music	tune
people	person
work	job
information	detail
weather	climate
furniture	sofa

6   **T.12.7.B.**

What delicious food!
What a delicious meal!
What lovely clothes!
What a lovely dress!
What varied work!
What a varied job!

8   **T.12.7.C.**

A sensible advice
B What sensible advice!

A foolish suggestion
B What a foolish suggestion!

A stale bread
B What stale bread!

A attractive furniture
B What attractive furniture!

A ugly sofa
B What an ugly sofa!

A monotonous music
B What monotonous music!

A smart luggage
B What smart luggage!

A horrible mess
B What a horrible mess!

A cold weather
B What cold weather!

A depressing information
B What depressing information!

A expensive rubbish
B What expensive rubbish!

A kind people
B What kind people!

A shabby dress
B What a shabby dress!

A disgusting meal
B What a disgusting meal!

8

2   **T.12.8.A.**

● ● ●	● ● ●
Superman	demanding
batteries	efficient
management	compulsive
habitat	rehearsal
certainly	achiever
everything	distracted
happening	creative
copyright	excuses

● ● ● ●	● ● ● ●
philosophy	Cinderella
abilities	occupation
unbearable	energetic
efficiently	
enjoyable	

3   **T.12.8.B.**

Hello there, Superman.
I've got a telegram
wishing you Happy Returns of
the day!
And there's some kryptonite
here in this parcel, so
now you're defenceless, and
can't run away.

Note: When Superman gets too
close to kryptonite, a green
stone which comes from his
home planet Krypton, he loses
all his superhuman powers.

Are you crying, Cinderella?
Don't be sorry,
Here's your chance:
With my magic
And your pumpkin
You will make it to the dance.

5   **T.12.8.C.**

●   ●
Aladdin was lazy.
    ●   ●
He never would learn.
    ●   ●
But now he's a rich man
      ●   ●
With money to burn.

    ●
Sir Lancelot
      ●
Loved Guinevere.
     ●
He blushed a lot
       ●
When she was near.

9

2　T.12.9.A.

    a.　the Colosseum
    b.　Buckingham Palace
    c.　the Eiffel Tower
    d.　the Statue of Liberty
    e.　Nelson's Column
    f.　the Pyramids
    g.　the Sphinx
    h.　the Victoria and Albert
       Museum
    i.　the Taj Mahal
    j.　St Paul's Cathedral
    k.　the Sistine Chapel
    l.　Westminster Abbey

5　T.12.9.B.

    a.　*Das Kapital*
    b.　the *Bible*
    c.　the *Odyssey*
    d.　*King Lear*
    e.　the Bayeux Tapestry
    f.　the Mona Lisa
    g.　the Venus de Milo
    h.　*Paradise Lost*
    i.　Michelangelo's David
    j.　*The Godfather*
    k.　*Don Quixote*
    l.　the *Koran*

7　a.　*Das Kapital*
    b.　*King Lear*
    c.　Nelson's Column
    d.　The Statue of Liberty
    e.　The Mona Lisa
    f.　The *Koran* . . . the *Bible*
    g.　The Bayeux Tapetry
    h.　The Sistine Chapel
    i.　St Paul's Cathedral
    j.　the Colosseum